"As a young girl, I dreamed of becoming a saint. I ran around our house with a slip on my head, hoping that if I could be good for *one day* then *someday* I might be good for more. It didn't quite turn out that way. Fast-forward fifty years and my firstborn has taken pen in hand to invite us into this wondrous life of more. He is a deeper thinker and writer than his mama. Obviously, I am proud. But it's more than that. In a time when so many young men are deconstructing the sacred, Addison has leaned into it. I am challenged, corrected, and lifted by *Saints: Becoming More Than 'Christians.'*"

**Lisa Bevere**, *New York Times* bestselling author
and ridiculously proud mother

"All I can say is 'Wow'! I expected an excellent literary work because Addison has excelled in academics all his life. But this 'Wow' speaks to the depth of knowledge, strength of wisdom, and keen insight found in *Saints*. Get ready—you will be confronted, encouraged, and challenged. It's obvious God has given Addison a voice, one that calls all generations to a higher level of living. As a father and fellow minister, I couldn't be prouder."

**John Bevere**, bestselling author and cofounder
of Messenger International

"Addison Bevere has a great mind and a good message. Through *Saints*, he encourages us to put on our identity as a saint and live in a relationship with Jesus. *Saints* is an authentic look at what faith can be."

**Bob Goff**, *New York Times* bestselling author
of *Love Does* and *Everybody, Always*

"Our lives are missing something as we traverse this world looking for fulfillment. We know that we are made for more than what we see, taste, and touch. In a profound and practical way, Addison Bevere points us to the only answer—Jesus. *Saints* is a clarion call to look past ourselves and to the only one who offers us the good life."

**Kyle Idleman**, senior pastor of Southeast Christian Church and author of *Not a Fan* and *Don't Give Up*

"Addison has done in *Saints* what every author endeavors to do—combine literary excellence with a truly original message. His writing is rich with new metaphors and creative illustrations, and his fun, often conversational delivery will keep you turning the pages till the end. His ability to mine new language and insight for the church will no doubt empower a generation to become what we're made to be—saints."

**Cory Asbury**, artist and songwriter of *Reckless Love*

"I read Addison Bevere's new book, *Saints*, with joy, and I tell you that it is jam-packed with insights about becoming the person God intended you to be. This book will challenge you, test you, possibly offend you at points—as every good book should—and cause you to think differently and be different if you act on what you read. *Saints* is on my list as highly recommended to my friends. Addison is not only a brilliant writer; he also gives us a brilliant message, one that is needed at this moment."

**Rick Renner**, Bible teacher, author, and founder of Renner Ministries and Moscow Good News Church

"Anyone worried about the spiritual health of millennials will be more than reassured by Addison Bevere's *Saints: Becoming More Than 'Christians.'* With depth, humor, wisdom, and insight into God's Word, Addison more than lives up to the legacy of his faith-filled parents, John and Lisa Bevere. While the word *Christian* seems to mean a lot of things to a lot of people, *Saints* calls us back to following our one and only, Jesus Christ."

**Chris Hodges**, senior pastor of Church of the Highlands and author of *The Daniel Dilemma* and *What's Next?*

"I truly believe that God's plans for each of us are far greater than we could ever ask, hope, or imagine. In *Saints: Becoming More Than 'Christians,'* Addison will encourage you to stop fighting for victory and start living from the victorious destiny we already have through Jesus."

**Christine Caine**, bestselling author
and founder of A21 and Propel Women

"Addison and the entire Bevere family have been close friends and colleagues for some time. I am honored to endorse Addison's new book, *Saints*. You will be encouraged, surprised, and blessed by his writings. I cannot wait to see where this project will lead and what doors the Lord will open moving forward—the sky's the limit!"

**Havilah Cunnington**, author, minister,
and founder of Truth to Table Ministries

"As I began reading *Saints* by Addison Bevere, I realized I was going to have to think more deeply about my relationship with God. This book has a classic feel and needs to be read by everyone who wants to take their life with Christ to another level!"

**Dennis Rouse**, senior pastor of
Victory World Church and author of *10*

"Addison Bevere has a unique voice in this generation. His new book is a force to be reckoned with in a world that misplaces its identity."

**Heather Lindsey**, author, speaker,
and founder of Pinky Promise

"Everything changes when you go through this step-by-step journey of becoming a saint and exploring God's otherness and what it means for our lives. Whoever reads this book will be transformed in their thinking and reshaped into their true spiritual identity."

**Rabbi Brian Bileci**, Simchat Yeshua Messianic Fellowship

"Sex! Success! Unending cash flow! Okay, so *Saints* might not be zeroing in on those salable topics, but I think you will be pleasantly surprised with what you find. To be honest, I wondered if this book would feel uberspiritual. You know, the kind that is so heavenly minded it feels no earthly good. I sure was wrong! So treat yourself to a good read. Empower your life with *Saints*!"

**Justin Mayo**, executive director of RedEye.org and YouthMentor.org

"Today, in a world obsessed with the status quo and fleeting vanity, we find ourselves in the middle of a historic identity crisis. Thank you, Addison, for quieting the noise of our culturally imposed, self-focused self-image and echoing what the Scriptures loudly declare—we are saints!"

**Scott Lindsey**, executive director of Faithlife (Logos Bible Software)

"In *Saints*, Addison Bevere brilliantly invites a generation that often reduces Christianity to moral codes or religious rituals into a far more compelling experience of truly knowing and following Christ. The power in his call to live as saints is underscored by the authenticity of his own intense pursuit of God and passion for truth. I'm honored to call him a friend and grateful for this important message."

**Dominic Russo**, founder of 1Nation1Day and Missions.Me

"With fresh illustrations and biblical insights, Addison opens our eyes to the thrill of being transformed by God. Read *Saints* cover to cover for your sake and because our generation desperately needs to see Jesus in us!"

**David Perkins**, lead pastor of Radiant Church

Saints

# Saints

## BECOMING MORE THAN "CHRISTIANS"

## ADDISON D. BEVERE

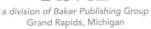

Revell

a division of Baker Publishing Group
Grand Rapids, Michigan

© 2020 by Addison D. Bevere

Published by Revell
a division of Baker Publishing Group
PO Box 6287, Grand Rapids, MI 49516-6287
www.revellbooks.com

Printed in the United States of America

Library of Congress Cataloging-in-Publication Data
Names: Bevere, Addison D., 1986– author.
Title: Saints : becoming more than "Christians" / Addison D. Bevere.
Description: Grand Rapids, MI : Revell, a division of Baker Publishing Group,
    [2019] | Includes bibliographical references.
Identifiers: LCCN 2019017719 | ISBN 9780800737009 (cloth)
Subjects: LCSH: Christian life.
Classification: LCC BV4501.3 .B479 2019 | DDC 248.4—dc23
LC record available at https://lccn.loc.gov/2019017719

Illustrations by Anna Cusack

The author is represented by The FEDD Agency, Inc.

20   21   22   23   24   25   26        7   6   5   4   3   2   1

green press INITIATIVE

*For Julianna*

# CONTENTS

# FOREWORD

I f you're anything like me, when you hear the word *saint*, you probably think of anybody but yourself. We picture stained glass windows depicting Peter, Paul, or Mary. We think of modern-day heroes like Mother Teresa who seem to transcend the rest of humanity. Yet the word *saint* is innately human; it tells the story of people so devoted to the person of Jesus that they served him with their whole selves, their true selves. The word *saint* has a deep-rooted history within the story of God's redemption and the fullness of life that he has for each one of us. A saint is someone who has been redeemed and found worthy by a perfect Savior.

The Bible refers to all believers as saints, yet we as a culture don't identify with that term. In this book, Addison Bevere brings this archaic term into the modern space as he invites us to reclaim and own the identity of saints as followers of Jesus. Addison's contagious curiosity and wonder will make you think of your identity in Christ in a new way. Claiming the identity of saint is not about how good a person each of us is—it is about the One who gave his life for us, who deserves our worship, who loves us in all our humanity. *Saints* is a charge to become more devoted followers of Jesus by encouraging us to expand our view of God and surrender our tendency toward self-worship and control. By expanding our view of God and allowing more space for wonder and mystery, we experience the world through God's divine perspective; we begin to see our lives as glorious moments of God's grace.

Addison Bevere's authentic and wholehearted pursuit of God makes him the perfect author of this message. Addison models the life of a saint by following the words and actions of Jesus, proving that devotion to Jesus is a transformative and glorious adventure. The message of *Saints* is not about achieving perfection but authentically and intimately walking with God as his plans for you are fully realized in your life. Through his book and through his life, Addison illuminates that devotion to God is not about a loss of self but rather a true understanding and full recognition of the person God created you to be.

Our identity in Christ is about embracing our true and whole selves so that God's glory can be revealed through us. Anything less is false humility, which is on par with pride. This book will challenge and awaken you to the higher calling that God has placed on your life. Sainthood is about a life of humble devotion and obedience; it is about the wonder and glory that can be found in every moment of every day as we walk with God.

*To all the saints reading this book,
grace and peace to you in Jesus Christ.*

*Mark Batterson*

# THE GOOD LIFE

*Good teacher, what must I do to experience life?*
*You know, the good life? —Mark 10:17*
*(my paraphrase)*

I recently found, hidden in plain sight, the secret formula for writing a bestselling book. Yes, you read that right. My discovery created a surge of power that I could hardly handle. It felt like learning the winning lottery numbers before the tickets had even been sold. Everything in my life was about to change.

Okay, I might've overstated a bit. It's bad form to begin with a lie, so I confess that I didn't actually find the secret sauce of publishing. But what I did discover is that many of the bestselling books have three things in common—three characteristics that undoubtedly help them climb bestseller lists and empty our wallets. Because I love books, I'm going to share my findings with you—just in case you want to write a bestseller one day.

First, use provocative language in your title—swearing is best. I could give some examples, but you get the idea.

Second, write a self-help book. People seem to like learning about themselves and finding ways to make themselves better. Go figure!

Third, include something about "the good life" in your title or subtitle. Those three words grouped together, in that order, seem to have a magical power. After all, isn't that what we all want? The good life.

If the good life could be turned into a product, *everyone* would want a piece of it. Nothing would be more profitable. Can you imagine selling such a thing? "Get your good life and find everything humankind has wanted since the beginning of time. Adam missed it. Plato couldn't find it. Nietzsche tried his best to give it words. The good life slipped through their fingers, but today you can have yours for a deal of a price!"

This may seem ridiculous and absurd, but entire industries (and religions) are built on our dissatisfaction with life. "Life-changing" products fly off assembly lines. We want the good life, and we're willing to pay for it. We'll drop thousands on anything that gives us even a taste of what we crave. (The credit card companies love this.)

The problem is we weren't created for just a nibble of the good life; we were designed to enjoy the whole thing. And until life reaches into the deepest regions of our being, we'll find ourselves disillusioned, annoyed, and victimized by the latest quack pushing life-changing gizmos and gadgets.

—I—

Our quest for the good life has led us into the information age. We are collecting and aggregating information at unprecedented rates, hoping that some data cluster will crack the code and unlock the next level of human existence. But there's just so much data. So many podcasts to listen to, books to read, TED Talks to watch, conferences to attend, people to meet, photos to take, experiences to have. With this abundance of data, how can we know when we're headed in the right direction?

Next time you're searching for a book online or in a store, take a look at some of the bestselling self-help books. You'll find books on organization, minimalism (my wife loves these), busyness, productivity, confidence, success, parenting, teamwork, sexuality, making money, managing money, investing money, printing money (you get the idea).

Many of these books have a promise. If you will just start doing *this*, your life will change for the better. One book will declare that less is the key to happiness, offering foolproof ways to manage your frantic pace of life and encouraging a divorce from busyness so you can enjoy an unhurried life, free from the tyrannies of incessant doing. But its shelf companion—collecting dust only inches away—will assert that more is, well, more, revealing never-before-heard-of tricks to do more with less time so you can accomplish more with the free time you have.

Hmm . . .

--‡--

As human beings, we're chronic pendulum swingers. Our lives get too busy, so we make work–life balance our singular pursuit. Or we find ourselves complacent and getting soft, so we find countless ways to energize our vocations and pursuits. Each month it's a new diet, a new scheduling technique, a new productivity app, a new parenting method, a new religious experience—the list has no end. We're chasing something we can never seem to catch. We're looking for something that's *other* than what we've known.

Now, don't get me wrong. I love learning new ideas and exploring great tools. From time to time I indulge in these "life-changing" products, and some actually do offer tips and tricks that help us manage our lives. But I've found that most products think too highly of their transformational power. They can help us manage life, but they cannot give life—even the best of them.

Despite their limited power, we still consume self-help books, TED Talks, courses, podcasts, and so on at a frantic pace. Why? Because we want what they promise. We want comfort, value, a good pace of life, success, better relationships, steamy marriages, kids who contribute to society. In other words, we want the good life. We want to feel alive. We want to be alive. But could it be that we're dissatisfied with what we've found because we're chasing shadows instead of pursuing the life we were made for?

Deep down, we know we are destined for more, and it drives us crazy.

## MORE TO LIFE

No matter how much we accomplish or experience, we all come back to this sense that *there has to be more to life*. And we're given a choice as we seek an answer. We can either build bigger, busying ourselves through greater exploits or distractions, or we can dig deeper, exploring the spiritual side of our humanity.

It doesn't take a genius to realize fulfillment isn't found in the conquest of the material world. Affluence and wealth do not guarantee happiness. And yet we spend much of our lives as slaves to our material gods.

Our other option is to come to a place where we acknowledge the existence of something greater *within* or *beyond* us—a transcendent source of the good life. But there's so much confusion in the spiritual world, the land of transcendence. As we dig deeper, we find that the word *spiritual* has been diluted to capture a variety of conflicting experiences, beliefs, and religions. It's been appropriated to prey on weak minds and desperate hearts. It's been detached from our everyday, material lives and often relegated to relics, holy buildings, or ephemeral fancies.

Even among Christians—a people group that supposedly represents almost one-third of the humans who call this planet home—there is contention around what our spiritual or religious lives should look like. You'll find countless opinions on how, practically speaking, our spirituality should shape our day-to-day lives.

Yet even in our differences, we Christians are all convinced that "humanity requires relationship with God before it can be itself."[1] In *A Guide for the Perplexed*, E. F. Schumacher reminded readers that "the scholastics used to say: *Homo non proprie humanus sed superhumanus est*—which means that to be properly human, you must go beyond the merely human."[2]

So what does it mean to go "beyond the merely human"? How do we tap into a new way of living that resonates with our irrepressible desire for something greater than what we've known? How do we find a hope that infuses us with a purpose and an identity that satisfies our souls?

We start with knowing this: we were created for goodness and perfection. That's why we innovate, progress, and change. But if our progress loses its purpose, it cannibalizes our humanity, leaving us distracted and disoriented. If innovation and change are not fulfilling our need to connect, to belong, to express, to love, to feel alive, how can they satisfy?

## DEATH FOR LIFE

Jesus, the hero of the world's most well-known spiritual narrative, offers us a mysteriously clear path to the good life: "Anyone who doesn't pick up their cross and follow after me doesn't deserve me. If you find your life you'll lose it, and if you lose your life because of me you'll find it" (Matt. 10:38–39).[3]

To paraphrase: die to self, follow him, and in this journey of losing your life, you'll find the life you were made for. At first glance, Jesus's words seem harsh and antilife—I mean, what's up with all this talk about death?

But Jesus is not being harsh. He's simply stating a fact. Outside of him there is no life—only existence. We were made for life—the God-infused life. Until we experience this kind of life and make it our pursuit, we will find ourselves hopelessly dissatisfied with the status quo.

In the first chapter of Matthew, we find a clear description of Jesus's purpose: he will save us from our sins, keeping us from "missing the true end and scope of life, which is God."[4]

With Christ comes the miraculous gift of rebirth—of new life—an awakening from a life of shadows. Though humanity was made in God's image, over the course of our existence, we relentlessly unmade ourselves. In our pursuit of life apart from God, we stripped ourselves from the source of life.

But God, the good Father, refused to let our mistake define us. In the greatest divine twist imaginable, he became a man to reclaim the life and purpose humanity had spurned. Jesus, the Son of God, fully man and fully God—not compromising his humanity or his divinity—has awakened our world from its slumber and offers us the chance to find the life we've been looking for.[5] Jesus said, "I am the bread of life; whoever comes to me shall not hunger" (John 6:35).

For thirty plus years, Jesus walked this earth as a human being, revealing the only way to do life. He was a real person. He traveled to real cities. He died on a hill with a name. But his time on earth was just the beginning. His example was catalytic and unprecedented, but alone it wasn't enough. If a mere model of right and wrong could engender change, his death would have been in vain. When he died, he sent his Spirit to teach us the intricacies of the art of living. That's why his Spirit is the only One who can fill our spiritual vacuum, helping us become truly human.

## WHAT MUST I DO?

You *know* you were created for more than what you see; God did, after all, put eternity in our hearts (Eccles. 3:1). There's an expansiveness inside us that cannot be denied.

That's why we're so eager to find a life that transcends what we now know. And while this eternal life is within us, it requires us to look beyond ourselves, admitting we're incomplete, which is not easy to do. Like Adam and Eve before us, we want to be like God apart from God. They were terrified of dependence, and so are we.

Let's look at one of Jesus's most famous conversations about finding life. This interaction was so memorable it was recorded in Matthew 19, Mark 10, and Luke 18. Each Gospel captures different facets of the story, so in places I've combined all three accounts.

Our narrative begins with an eager young man. He is wealthy and possesses great status. He's young, rich, and famous. In other words, he's living the good life. Luke's Gospel gives us reason to believe he was also a synagogue official, a member of the religious elite. It's evident this man was important. And it's probable his fraternizing with the likes of Jesus was discouraged among his peers.

Yet here we find him in the dirt and on his knees, in public mind you, begging Jesus for answers. Mark's account also reveals that he ran to Jesus. In Jewish culture, such running was disgraceful and unfit for a man of his status. Clearly, this man was desperate and willing to discard decorum's demands. Upon capturing Jesus's attention, he implores, "Good Teacher, what good deed must I do to have eternal life?"[6]

Let's break down this question. First, the rich young man (Richie, for short) honors Jesus by calling him teacher. He also sees Jesus as a good man, so he appeals to his goodness. Clearly, he respects Jesus and believes Jesus is capable of giving him the answer he seeks. Otherwise, Richie wouldn't risk his dignity. Remember, this is risky business for someone of Richie's stature. Jesus is, after all, an unlearned man, a lowly carpenter.

Second, notice that Richie believes eternal life can be obtained by an act of goodness—and more specifically, an act of goodness performed by him.

Third, notice who the hero is. Based on how Richie positions his inquiry, he, once discovering the truth, would be the hero, the one who would right the ship. Jesus, the teacher, would point him in the right direction, but Richie would do all the heavy lifting.

Fourth, this man is seeking eternal life, something he has not attained but greatly desires. Richie, like all of us, has an innate dissatisfaction with the life he's known. I believe his desire was to experience qualities of the eternal in the temporal. As an educated first-century Jew, he would have been very familiar with the promise of God's Messiah and the eternal kingdom—a kingdom marked by peace, wholeness, and prosperity.

With that in mind, let's see how Jesus responds to such a noble request from this distinguished man: "Why do you call me good? No one is good except God alone. If you would enter life, keep the commandments."[7]

I've always been puzzled by Jesus's response. It seems that Jesus is saying that he, the Son of God, is not good. But isn't Jesus one with the Father? So if the Father is good, wouldn't Jesus be good? And if Jesus and the Father are one, is not Jesus's response misleading at best and a lie at worst?

Let's reframe the interaction by answering this question: Is Richie appealing to the goodness of Jesus's humanity or the goodness of his divinity? Richie sees Jesus as merely human, so Jesus answers as any human must: "No one is good except God alone." Yes, Jesus was and is both God and man, but Richie saw only humanity. I'm confident Richie would have received a different answer if he had appealed to Jesus's divinity. As it was, Richie was not looking for a God to save him—he was looking for a man to teach him.

So Jesus plays Richie's game. Richie wants to use his goodness to access life, and Jesus indulges him by quoting the good law: "Do not murder, do not commit adultery, do not steal, do not bear false witness, do not defraud, honor your father and mother, love your neighbor as yourself."[8]

Notice that Jesus identifies only behaviors, those that are evident to others. He doesn't address the condition of Richie's heart. He also doesn't reference any of the vertical commandments—the ones that cover our relationship with God.

Richie's next words reveal that his own perceived goodness was the god of his heart—an idol that he drew strength from. We now see that Richie was trying to leverage his goodness to save himself from the futility and emptiness of life apart from God's Spirit. He says, "All these I have kept from my youth. What do I still lack?"[9]

We now see both frustration and contempt in Richie's response. He's frustrated because Jesus isn't giving him anything new. He's contemptuous because Jesus is offering instructions that he apparently mastered when he was a wee child.

Here's the important question for us to ask ourselves: Why wasn't Richie relieved by Jesus's response? If he had indeed followed Jesus's counsel, then he was set. He had kept the law. Based on what Jesus said, eternal life was his, right?

But Richie knew there was more. He had mastered human goodness, yet it had failed to make him good. It had failed to perfect his soul. Deep down, he knew he was wretched. He knew he wasn't experiencing the promised life. He wrestled with emptiness and purposelessness. Richie had summited the mountain of human perfection and found it devoid of anything great. He could also sense that the only thing his climb had achieved was an awareness of an infinitely greater climb that still stood before him—one that would require something new. Something different. Something other and more than who he had been and what he had been doing since he was a child. But Jesus wasn't giving him what he needed to scale the great mountain of goodness, and Richie couldn't shake the sense that he still lacked something.

How does Jesus respond to Richie's frustration? With love. Jesus loves him by speaking heaven's language in words Richie can understand: "If you would be perfect, go, sell what you possess and give to the poor, and you will have treasure in heaven; and come, follow me."[10]

Richie is sorrowed by Jesus's response, but I think he saw it coming. Jesus pinpointed a lack of goodness that our friend had been able to hide. Yes, Richie wanted to experience eternal life, but he could not separate himself from the comforts of his present position. To give up his goods would be to part from his identity. At that time, one did not have status without wealth. Richie's wealth and possessions made him appear good in the eyes of others. He was still the hero of his story, so he needed to appear good. And what good is a man who has nothing?

Jesus brought him to the brink of death—death to self—and offered a ticket into the perfect life, the good life. But the man could not take the ticket—he couldn't take the ticket because it came from someone else. He wanted to be the master of his fate, the grantor of his goodness, and the prince of his perfection. He wasn't looking for a Lord and Savior; he was looking for a good teacher. So "when the young man heard this he went away sorrowful, for he had great possessions."[11]

✦I✦

How could Jesus let this man get away? Wasn't he a prime candidate for building God's kingdom? Did he not possess great status and resources that could be leveraged to impact lives for the gospel? Sure, he was a bit full of himself and too attached to stuff, but Jesus could fix our rich friend, right?

Everyone including the disciples were in shock. They probably compared themselves to Richie and found themselves lacking. Remember, these were the guys who constantly competed to be the greatest. I imagine Peter was threatened when Jesus invited Richie to follow him. This man seemed to have it all going for him: wealth, godliness, status, passion. But he went away because of his imperfection.

By the time Richie came onto the scene, the disciples had made a lot of mistakes, and Jesus wasn't reluctant to point them out. These guys were a mess. That's why when Richie is dismissed, the disciples ask Jesus, "Who then can be saved?" (Matt. 19:25). In other words, "This guy was more perfect than any of us. Are we not to inherit eternal life?!"

Jesus replies to them, "With man this is impossible, but with God all things are possible" (v. 26).

Eternal life cannot be accessed by our goodness but by receiving God's goodness. No matter how good we make ourselves, we cannot become what we were created to be. And we won't experience the good life we all want until we drink from its source. Likely Richie went home to his wealth, possessions, and status only to discover that he had tasted life and rejected it.

## THE THING BEFORE THE THING

Some people mistakenly believe the story of the rich young man is just about getting rid of wealth or material goods. But here's the thing: possessions are merely tools. They are neither inherently good nor inherently bad.

The thing Jesus wanted Richie to do was follow him. Selling his possessions was just the thing before the thing. Jesus knew the only way for this man to discover the good life was to follow him and learn the nuances and otherworldly subtleties of the God life—the life that gives up everything to have the one thing worth having. Richie's possessions were holding him back; Jesus offered freedom from their control.

Keep in mind, Jesus did not require all his followers to sell everything they had and give their possessions to the poor. Upon Jesus's death, one of his disciples—Joseph of Arimathea—was granted an audience with Pilate, the Roman governor of Judea. Joseph was able to convince Pilate to let him bury Jesus's body in his own tomb. I have no doubt that he paid a high price for Jesus's body. In fact, the Bible calls Joseph "a rich man" (Matt. 27:57).

The point is that possessions can neither give nor take away life. They are products of life, not life itself.

We all have things before the thing. Things that keep us from experiencing what will make us come alive. Things that keep us from trading our lives for what matters most. Things that keep us from following Jesus and learning from him. To find life, you must place these things—your career, family, money, dreams, success, relationships—in their proper place. These things, while good, aren't capable of taking you where you want to go. They do, however, travel well on the back of something greater.

## CRIMINAL

A thief—let's call him Criminal—finds himself on death's door. A lifetime of pain and disappointment plays in the theater of his mind. He has wasted his life violating others and is now found unworthy to live.

Out of the corner of his eye, he spots an outlet for his anguish. Desperate to numb his pain, he hurls insults at a guy named Jesus, the "King of the Jews."[12] I imagine Criminal thinking, *I might be a criminal, but at least I don't pretend to be the Son of God. This Jesus is even worse than me.*

But then something happens. Criminal sees Jesus do something he'd never seen before. He watches the Son of God cry out for the forgiveness of his tormentors, even while they hurl insults and inflict unthinkable pain. In an instant, Criminal's eyes open—what he's seeing is beyond human.

Criminal realizes he has a front-row seat to the execution of Life itself.

Jesus's followers have hidden from the cross. Whether out of fear or pain, they can't stomach watching their Messiah murdered. But Criminal has no choice. His proximity puts him in the throes of grotesque glory. I imagine him, despite his pain, being transfixed by the Holy One. But then he's awakened from his daze. *What are these new insults I hear?* he thinks. He looks over to see the other criminal still mocking the Son of God. And this criminal isn't just mocking Jesus; he's also mocking his saving power—the very reason Jesus is on the cross.

I love Criminal's indignation:

"Do you not fear God, since you are under the same sentence of condemnation? And we indeed justly, for we are receiving the due reward of our deeds; but this man has done nothing wrong." And he said, "Jesus, remember me when you come into your kingdom." (Luke 23:40–42)

These are this man's final moments. Breath will soon leave his body. Yet here we find him giving his last heave to defend innocence and request forgiveness. Criminal has become a new man. And at death's door, he has found new life—a life that can even energize his death.

How will Jesus respond to Criminal's swan song? This desperate cry from the man who was unfit to live? Jesus says to him, "Truly, I say to you, today you will be with me in paradise" (v. 43).

+―+

Criminal, just like the rich young man, sought the path to eternal life. But Criminal had no goodness to hold on to. He wasn't looking for a good teacher. He knew he needed a Savior. Two men, one pursuit, two very different responses.

So many of us miss out on life because we're looking for a better version of what we've known. But the good life we all crave is paradoxical—death to find life—and reaches beyond the wisdom of this world. And here's the reason: God's not interested in just giving us a better life. He's not a self-help guru who's looking to make a quick buck off our nominal improvement. God's in the business of lasting, holistic transformation for the sake of eternal vocation. He has given us a calling, identity, and community that reach beyond the here and now. Our souls long for this new way of living. It's too spacious for our world's temporal fillings. There's a new life that is found only in the awakening of our True Self.

That's why the good life isn't *something* you find; it's *someone* you become.

And it starts here, now. This new life dignifies time, space, and matter, igniting them with purpose. God loves our material world. He calls it good. He celebrates our advances in medicine, science, engineering, teaching, and so on. But there's more than what we can build with our hands. And in the discovery of this *more*, our True Self comes alive in hope, promise, and purpose.

In the arms of this new life, you will find the power and the perspective to rise above the limitations of your present world and its ideas of goodness. By the power of God's eternal Spirit, you can become a Saint: someone whose life is marked by a hope and a purpose that astound our world and point people to the One who is life.

But here's the thing: we will not find the good life until we leave our notions of goodness behind. Paradoxically, once we reject our understanding of the good life, we will find ourselves overcome by new life. As we yield to the magnitude of this new way of being, losing our smallness in God's largeness, we will become people who participate in the mystery of life.

We will become Saints.

# SAINTS

*God creates out of nothing. . . .*
*But he does what is still more wonderful:*
*he makes saints out of sinners.* —Søren Kierkegaard

This book is not a story of the canonized saints of old. If you are looking for such a book, I apologize for the inconvenience and will not be offended if you decide to send this book back to wherever it came from. I do believe, however, that if we work together, we can breathe new life into an ancient term, giving it necessary relevance and power in our quest for life.

At first glance, you may have struggled with this book's subtitle: *Becoming More Than "Christians."* Please understand that I'm not campaigning against the term *Christian*. Truth be told, it's not a bad identifier. But it has become too familiar, too cheap. "Jesus" and "Christ" are ubiquitous in speech and not always in a good sense. As Westerners, we're more or less all cultural Christians, especially in the conservative pockets of society. But the collective identity of *Christian* has been homogenized and turned into a nightmare of unrecognizable gruel, like the stuff lunch ladies plop onto the plates of terrified children.

The food is certainly "inclusive," but it lacks any form or definition because it is everything—thousands of leftovers combined—and yet nothing. Sadly, the term *Christian* suffers the same fate. I suggest looking elsewhere for a term that captures the mystery of our new life in Christ, our promised True Self.

While the identifier *Christian* is used only three times in the New Testament, *hagios*—translated as "saints"—is used over sixty times. According to *HarperCollins Bible Dictionary*, *hagios* "refers to those whose relationship with God is maintained through faith in Jesus Christ."[1] At first glance, this definition doesn't seem any different from what we would call a Christian. Based on this accurate (yet incomplete) definition, every person who has a relationship with God through faith in Jesus Christ is a Saint. You don't have to be born with stars over your crib—all of us are invited to enjoy this ever-growing, faith-empowered relationship with the One who is Life.

+I+

This invitation to be a Saint was a vital part of the early church's language and identity. That's why Paul would often begin his letters by addressing his audience as Saints.

To all those in Rome who are loved by God and called to be saints. (Rom. 1:7)

To those sanctified in Christ Jesus, called to be saints together with all those who in every place call upon the name of our Lord Jesus Christ. (1 Cor. 1:2)

To the saints and faithful brothers in Christ at Colossae.
(Col. 1:2)

Just by surveying these three verses, we can safely surmise
that all of us are called to be Saints. And when God calls us
to do or become something, he provides the means. Like
any good father, God doesn't enjoy watching us flounder,
but he does give us space and opportunity to learn and grow.
What's mind-boggling is we get to partner with God as we
discover the depths of his plans for us. These verses also
show us death is not a prerequisite for sainthood. Not only
can we become Saints in this lifetime, but we are also expected to embrace this identity and bring its corresponding
reality into this world.

While I like *HarperCollins Bible Dictionary*'s definition,
I'm not a fan of their use of the word *maintained*: "Refers to
those whose relationship with God is maintained through
faith in Jesus Christ."

A relationship can't be maintained through faith. I think
"grown" or "enlarged" or "awakened" should replace
"maintained"; basically, I'm looking for something expansive. After all, life shouldn't be about maintenance.
It's about expansion. A small view of this journey in
Christ—to realizing our True Self—is responsible for the
lack of imagination and transformation found in Chris-
tendom today. I've certainly found this to be true in my
own life.

The baseline definition of *hagios* is a personal relationship
with God through faith in his Son, Jesus Christ. There is
nothing wrong with that primary definition. We cannot

experience the life God has for us without first recognizing and embracing this foundation. But there's more to being a Saint.

The *Tyndale Bible Dictionary* adds that saints "are the people of the coming age."[2] In other words, *a saint is someone who brings a future reality into the present.* They transcend the problems and limitations of the temporal by embracing and partnering with the eternal. They find elements of the promised life of God's coming age—the age when God is known and seen by all—and by partnering with God's Spirit, they bring evidence of that age into the very real problems and opportunities in our world today.

Saints aren't people who escape from the real world, living detached from the struggles of life. To become a Saint is to become profoundly human. It's to plunge into God's original design for humanity. It's to feel what God feels for this world, empowering us to align our actions with his heart. It's to embrace God's nature and to step into the fullness of our new creation reality. The Son of God became a man to make men and women sons and daughters of God,[3] and Saints have caught a glimpse of who they are in Christ. They possess a hope and a confidence in God's promise to make all things new and purposefully work with his Spirit to bring that future reality into the present.

Prior to Jesus's death, the evidence of heaven's reality—the ultimate future reality—was limited for the most part to the temple. And only the priests were granted access to what was then heaven's microcosm on earth.

But now God's people, his Saints, are his temple. Everywhere we go, we can bring heaven's reality with us: "Do you not know that you are God's temple and that God's Spirit dwells in you? . . . God's temple is holy, and you are that temple" (1 Cor. 3:16–17).

When we awaken to the Spirit's work in our lives, we create thin places, spots where the veil between the two dimensions—heaven and earth—is incredibly thin. Spots where God's final Word becomes evident in our world. Our prayer "on earth as it is in heaven" becomes a reality.

When I reference heaven, please don't think just of a celestial city. We, as Saints, can experience many of heaven's realities—peace, joy, togetherness, forgiveness, love, mercy, wholeness, justice, and so on—in our lives today, revealing heaven to a world desperate for something more.

Heaven is indeed a real place in a different dimension. I'm not saying that it isn't. Jesus did tell Criminal that on that day he would join Jesus in paradise. But God's plan has always been to bring heaven to earth. That's the end goal as revealed in Scripture. And our lives, energized here and now by the power of the Spirit, are part of the promise that God is making all things new (Rev. 21:5).

## GREEN EGGS AND GOD

> For by grace you have been saved through faith. And this is not your own doing; it is the gift of God. (Eph. 2:8)

My kids (I have four of them) love the book *Green Eggs and Ham* by Dr. Seuss. Even today, it's one of the favorites in our home. My son Asher used to ask me to read it every night. I've read it so many times that, at one point, I had memorized all the words. I'm about to do some serious exegetical work here, so I can't just assume you've read this classic. Here's a short recap for those of you who haven't read it or need a refresher.

The book has two main characters: Sam-I-Am and the grumpy old man. Their journey begins with Sam asking Grumpy if he likes green eggs and ham. Grumpy vehemently denies any desire to try such distasteful food, but Sam is not discouraged. He quickly proposes that a change of scenery could change Grumpy's opinion of the green delicacy.

With every few pages, new scenery emerges. You'll find them in a house, with a fox, on a train, in the rain, on a boat, and eventually in a large body of water. But despite Sam's persistence, Grumpy maintains his unwillingness to try the food. Finally, after finding himself nearly drowned, Grumpy agrees to try the food just to get Sam off his back. This is, after all, now a matter of life and death.

Much to his surprise, Grumpy ends up loving greens eggs and ham and spends the rest of the book telling Sam that he would eat it in all the places that he previously said he would not. And that's the book. (Fun fact: the book uses only fifty unique words because Dr. Seuss wanted to win a bet with his editor.)

One night, after reading this simple narrative again, God showed me something that has forever changed my life. As I was praying for my kids and tucking them into bed, God whispered this into my spirit: *I'm a lot like Sam.* At first I didn't get it. But after some consideration, I thought I knew what God was trying to tell me. "Yeah," I whispered, "you're like Sam in the sense that you continue to offer your gift of salvation to humanity despite its disinterest."

I could sense that my guess wasn't wrong, but I knew it was incomplete. So I asked God to show me what I was missing. He soon revealed that Grumpy is not a symbol for the world but rather a symbol for me. He showed me that the gift of salvation is the most wonderfully multifaceted gift that's ever been given. Yet I've refused to unpack many of its facets that seem foreign or don't necessarily suit my fancy.

He then showed me how he uses changes of scenery in my life to arrest my attention and change my perspective. In that moment, I became deeply aware of God's patience. Despite my ignorance and resistance, he faithfully keeps giving me chances to understand and welcome the reach of his saving power.

I was hooked.

I wanted to know more about this gift of salvation. I didn't want to confine it to comfort in the afterlife or condemnation-free living in the present—I wanted to know more about what it means to be saved by grace through faith.

The only way we can experience the life we all long for, the life that is woven into the fabric of our being, is to reimagine what it means to be saved by grace through faith.

## SOLA GRATIA

> The gospel, which has come to you, as indeed in the whole world . . . is bearing fruit and increasing—as it also does among you, since the day you heard it and understood the grace of God in truth. (Col. 1:5–6)

Grace. We love talking, singing, and writing about grace. It's miraculous. Grace does what we could never do. Grace goes where we could never go.

There's been a resurgence of grace teachings over the last ten to fifteen years. These teachings have helped many people move past condemnation and shame, which is a good thing. Growing up, I remember feeling like I needed to get saved every time I went to church. The messages were harsh, and I think the preachers measured success based on how many people rededicated their lives during the service. I left most services believing God was just looking for a reason to send me to hell.

In fact, when I was eight or nine, I became terrified that I might grow up to be the antichrist. This might seem like a ridiculous fear, but it was real to me.

Almost every time I snuck TV time without my parents' knowledge (we weren't allowed to watch much TV), I inevitably stumbled upon a show or movie with exorcism or devil worship. I thought that maybe this was the devil's way of circumventing my parents' angelic safeguards to send me coded messages and instructions. I would quickly change the channel, but the images wouldn't leave my mind. And then there's my birthdate, which has three 6s in it. And everyone knows that's the devil's number.

The combination of scary preaching, demonic shows, and the numbers on my birth certificate created the perfect conditions for my incessant nightmares. At one point, I finally told my mom my secret fear because I couldn't handle the late-night terrors.

My mom probably had a hard time not laughing, but somehow she kept a straight face and quickly informed me that she too has three 6s in her birthdate. For a brief second, I considered the chances of her being the antichrist (sorry, Mom), but I quickly dismissed that notion.

My mom also explained that the mere fact I didn't want to be the antichrist was a telltale sign that I wasn't the cursed one. It took me a while, but I was eventually able to see things her way.

Obviously, this was not a healthy way for me to view myself or God. Our heavenly Father doesn't want us to live in fear. In fact, the most repeated command in Scripture is "do not fear." God wants us to live with courage and faith, expecting his best for our lives. We are told to approach his throne, the throne of grace, with boldness. Not because of anything we've done but because of who he is. We are worthy of this grace because of what Jesus did—our worthiness is a derivative of his. "Let us then with confidence draw near to the throne of grace, that we may receive mercy and find grace" (Heb. 4:16).

God's not trying to hide grace from us; he wants to overwhelm us with it. As John's Gospel says, "For from his fullness we have all received, grace upon grace" (1:16). Grace upon grace. Multiplied grace is what we're talking about. God's transcendent grace is available to you without measure. When reading the New Testament, you'll notice the majority of the letters begin with a blessing of grace. Peter even writes, "May grace and peace be multiplied to you" (1 Pet. 1:2). Grace is a good thing, and it comes from a good Father.

—I—

You might have heard people comment that there is too much teaching on grace in the church today, and this imbalance gives people a license to sin without feeling bad. I've heard people refer to these grace teachers and their teachings as hyper or extreme grace.

In truth, we haven't come close to the extremities or hyperstate of grace's nature. The words *hyper* and *extreme* imply a measure that is greater than reality. If grace emanates from the fullness of God, then there's no way we could exhaust its depths. We need more teaching on the grace of God, not less.

We've actually undersold grace, and grace that is undersold leads to sloppy grace. A grace devoid of imagination. A grace that saves you from hell in the future but abandons you to hell here and now. A grace that presents a cure for the human condition but then throws that cure out the window. Such a grace, and such a gospel, is not worthy of our God.

Grace can open our eyes to the True Self, the life we have in Christ *now*: "It is no longer I who live, but Christ who lives in me" (Gal. 2:20). In Christ, we have a new identity, and we will not experience the life we were made for until we embrace this identity. The False Self must be crucified so the True Self, infused with Christ's Spirit, can emerge.

> Whoever wants to be my disciple must deny themselves and take up their cross and follow me. For whoever wants to save their life will lose it, but whoever loses their life for me will find it. What good will it be for someone to gain the whole world, yet forfeit their soul? (Matt. 16:24–26 NIV)

Jesus repeatedly tells us that we find life only in death. On the surface, this cryptic remark seems contradictory. But it makes perfect sense when we understand that each of us has a False Self (or Old Self) and a True Self (or New Self). In Colossians 3:9–10, Paul writes, "Put off the old self with its practices and . . . put on the new self, which is being renewed in knowledge after the image of its creator."

I think of the Old Self as pseudoindividuality. It may look like individuality, but it's just a shadow of the unique brilliance God intends for each of us. As usual, C. S. Lewis articulates this beautifully:

> The more we get what we now call "ourselves" out of the way and let Him take us over, the more truly ourselves we become. There is so much of Him that millions and millions of "little Christs," all different, will still be too few to express Him fully. . . . Our real selves are all waiting for us in Him. It is when I . . . g[a]ve myself up to His Personality, that I first began to have a real personality of my own.

Until you have given up your self to Him you will not have a real self. Sameness is to be found most among the most "natural" men. . . . How gloriously different are the saints.[4]

In Christ, we don't lose our individuality. We find it—reborn and infused with God's DNA. If we are to become Saints, we must let go of the Old Self. There is no middle ground.

Sloppy grace refuses to acknowledge our new creation reality in Christ. It will pacify or manage the False Self but not awaken our True Self. Sloppy grace causes people to reduce the gospel to moralism, making people feel condemned for not living as they should. Alternatively, it allows them to create a self-focused reality in which how they live doesn't matter because Jesus was righteous for them. Both extremes release the individual from any love-oriented, missional responsibility that extends beyond the confines of a small, False Self existence.

Let me make something very clear: we will not feel alive until we align ourselves with the person and the work of Life. The True Self—which is a transcendent harmony of both God and us—is a river of life that only expands as it flows.

Don't allow a false grace to make your life small. Grace enlarges our lives, introducing a greater vision of who we are in Christ. This vision will create tension, but that's okay. With vision comes hope, and you cannot have hope without tension. In fact, the only way to eradicate tension is to abandon hope, and a life without hope is no life at all.

We need to live in the tension. Through pain and joy we will awaken to the God-within life. That is the design and purpose of God's grace. It connects us to the person of Jesus, positioning us to feel what he felt and do what he did. We will never do the greater works that Jesus spoke of (John 14:12) until we abandon our False Self and put on our True Self, re-created in his righteousness and holiness (Eph. 4:21–24).

The gospel—the good news, the revelation of God's grace—will reshape our world when we, as Christ's people, his ambassadors on the earth, understand "the grace of God in truth" (Col. 1:6). In other words, lives will change when we're willing to welcome grace in all its beauty and wonder. And to do that, we'll have to go beyond ourselves and tap into the mysteries of the cross and its implications in our lives.

> This is the wonderful message that is . . . powerfully changing hearts throughout the earth, just like it has changed you! Every believer of this good news *bears the fruit of eternal life* as they experience the reality of God's grace. (Col. 1:6 TPT, emphasis added)

## THE FOOD

My whole life I've been in church. My parents are ministers and authors who have written more than thirty books between them. I've traveled with them all over the world. Throughout the years, I've had intimate conversations with some of the greatest pastors, authors, and Christian thinkers of our time. I've sat at their tables, played their golf courses, and prayed in their green rooms. I've been able to see so much, and I think these experiences have given me a desire for more.

But many people who grow up in Christian homes become disillusioned with the church. More and more young Christians leave the church as they enter adulthood.[5] And from what I've seen, it's not any better for those of us who spent most of our childhood literally in the church because of our parents' employment. Being on the "inside," we saw things, things we can't unsee. And after seeing what went down in the kitchen, many of us decide not to eat the food.

But, in reality, the kitchen is not the sustenance. It's a place that prepares, packages, and presents sustenance, but it's not the food. We shouldn't refuse sustenance because of a bad experience with a kitchen. This is the same as refusing to eat because you once had a bad experience at a certain restaurant.

＋I＋

As we move forward, I invite you to ask God's Spirit to remove any prejudices or preconceived ideas that could keep you from eating the food and experiencing the life God has for you. These mindsets could have been caused by dynamics at home, church, school, or work. But the very things the enemy uses to diminish our view of God and the life he has for us, God can and will redeem to bring us into the richness and fullness of salvation.

Regardless of where you've been, or what you've seen or done, today is a new day. God's promises *are* alive and active in your life. But first you must believe in their existence, then you can experience their power.

# MIRROR, MIRROR

For the longest time, I viewed salvation and conversion as synonymous. I thought of salvation as that moment when I worked up the courage to go down to the altar to give my life to Jesus. I know this may seem odd, but I believed that was the apex of the Christian experience. From that point forward, I figured my goal was to hold on to my altar experience and do my best to be a good Christian.

Then God showed me that conversion was only the beginning of salvation's work in my life and that my making conversion synonymous with salvation could be compared to making the start of a marathon synonymous with its middle and end. I learned that while the start is very important, an unhealthy infatuation with a starting line will keep one from running a race and experiencing the joys and thrills of the journey.

Conversion is salvation's starting line. But salvation is much more than conversion.

Do we need a starting line? Absolutely. Should we celebrate the starting line? Of course. Scripture says a myriad of angels celebrates the moment a sinner first turns from their ways. But is there more? Yes! And the little book of James opened my eyes to that *more*.

## JESUS'S BROTHER

The gift of salvation is first and foremost a change of identity. When we understand this truth, the New Testament will make much more sense. When we discover that our salvation promises to infuse us with the divine, turning us into sons and daughters of God, then we'll begin to look at God's Word and ways in a new light.

There's a reason James became the leader of the church in Jerusalem, and that reason wasn't nepotism. James did life with the One who is Life (John 14:6). As the brother of Jesus, James no doubt saw things that made him question what it is to be human—things that made him uncomfortable with easy answers and half-truths. His proximity to Jesus created a depth in him, a depth that eventually turned into profound respect and love for Jesus as the Son of God and Savior of his soul.

James's lofty view of Jesus led him to pen these words: "Receive with meekness the implanted word, which is able to save your souls" (James 1:21). These thirteen words are loaded with hope and promise, and they abound with meaning. Notice that this is a charge, an imperative statement. James is not passively suggesting we receive the implanted word. He is firmly telling us to do so. Also, this instruction lies within the first few paragraphs of his letter, which means this truth is foundational and necessary if the reader is to understand the rest of his message.

James makes it clear throughout this letter that his message is intended for people who are following Jesus. It's a manifesto on how to be the people of God *for* the people of God.

Returning to James 1:21, we read, "Receive with [humility] the implanted word, which is able to save your souls." I substituted *humility* for *meekness*. Some versions use *humility*, and this word is more widely understood today. When I think of childlikeness, humility is the first attribute that comes to mind. Kids love learning and exploring new things. They are rarely satisfied with shallow answers because their imaginations know no bounds. Regardless of how many answers you give them, there's always a follow-up question, especially after they've been put to bed and their minds are reframing information gathered throughout their day.

At times, bedtime in our home feels like a reverse hostage situation: we're giving our four kids whatever they want to get them to *stay* in their rooms. It baffles me how many questions they have when I'm putting them to bed. My wife and I will be in our room and suddenly we hear a pitter-patter growing louder. Knock, knock, knock. Sure enough, another kid is out of bed with a question such as "Why do bad things happen to good people and shouldn't God just stop bad things from happening?" Despite my wishing otherwise, you can't just leave a question like that unanswered. Not to mention the answer is difficult and will invariably lead to many follow-up questions.

But God never gets frustrated by our questions. In fact, he invites us to be relentless in our asking (Matt. 7:7–11; Luke 11:9–13). An inquisitive disposition will lead to a greater understanding of truth, and he is the truth. A life of childlike humility will give us eyes to see who God is and what he has for us.

Jesus constantly mentioned the idea of having eyes to see. His countrymen were looking for a warring Messiah to save them from Roman oppression, but instead, Jesus offered a freedom that can be found and grown in the midst of oppression. This is why he continually spoke of seeing the world and ourselves in a new light. It's also why all the Gospels begin with John the Baptist preaching repentance, which is ultimately a change of perception that leads to a new way of living and a new identity.

The good news is we don't need a new landscape; we don't need our environment to change before our lives can change. We can experience peace, wholeness, and grace in the midst of turmoil, pain, and injustice. God's saving power supersedes circumstance; it's not hampered by the latest tragedy. But we must chase it with humility, knowing our journey will test the limits of our imagination and redefine our view of "impossible."

## BEYOND THE BEGINNING

Again, James says, "Receive with humility the implanted word, which is able to save your souls." Let's now turn our attention to this idea of the *implanted word*.

When I was young, I loved Michael Jordan. I was convinced that I'd be a professional basketball player one day (this was after I got past the fear that I might be the antichrist). I'd practice every day with my neighbors, and I became quite the little baller.

When I was ten, I won a door-sized poster of Michael Jordan palming a basketball while flying through space. (It was my prize for shamelessly begging neighbors to purchase magazines they would never read.) I used to sit in my room and stare at the poster, dreaming about spending quality time with my gravity-defying bestie. In fact, I used to speak to the poster and engage Michael in all sorts of interesting dialogue. (I guess they were actually monologues.)

Then one day my dad took away my poster. He said I was obsessed and needed to rethink my love for Michael Jordan. I'm convinced he thought I was praying to the poster. We lived in a small house, so it's possible he heard my murmurs and mistook them for prayers to the basketball god.

I was devastated. MJ was my hero, my idol. And my dad was Gideon, determined to cleanse our house of idol worship. But what my dad forgot was that I had a Michael Jordan Russian doll hidden in my sock drawer. It was actually my younger brother's, but I had exercised older brother rights and claimed it as my own. (For the record, I've since given it back to Austin.)

As you likely know, a Russian doll is the gift that keeps on giving. These little people keep popping out, until they don't. That's the sad part of it all. Once they've been unpacked, you don't really know what to do with the dolls. Not to mention they look weird when they're split in half, like someone who's been victimized by a lousy street magician.

For the longest time, I viewed the gift of salvation like a Russian doll. Conversion could be likened to that moment when I first held the Michael Jordan goodness. For a few minutes, I sat there admiring the intricacies of his design. I couldn't believe how blessed I was. My world had changed with MJ's arrival.

But after a while, I wanted to see who else was inside Michael. Pop! I knew whom I would find, but that didn't keep me from being excited to see Scottie Pippen.

Scottie Pippen was an amazing basketball player and a Hall of Famer. But he wasn't Michael Jordan, so I didn't spend as much time admiring that doll. It wasn't long before I wanted to see who was inside Scottie. Pop! Out came Dennis Rodman with green hair. Like Scottie, Dennis was a great basketball player, but he didn't hold a candle to MJ or Scottie. Pop! Tony Kukoc was next. I didn't know much about him except that he's Croatian. Pop! Out came the final doll, Steve Kerr. Steve was so small I could hardly read his name on the jersey.

With each pop, I found myself less satisfied. I knew the best was already behind me. The greatness of the gift diminished with time, and the dolls found themselves sitting on a shelf or in a sock drawer, locked away inside Michael Jordan, the only truly special part of the lot.

Isn't that how it is with so many things in life? We step into something with great anticipation—a job, a marriage, a friendship, raising kids—only to find the beginning was the best part.

Happy couples commemorate their union with joy and unbridled adoration, yet within several years, many of them can be found spewing insults in a vacuous conference room, every action controlled by conniving divorce attorneys. We celebrate the purchase of a new car, posting pictures so our friends can share in our jubilation. But after six months, there's food strewn across the back seat, and Betsy (seems like a good car name) is in desperate need of a wash. Many of us begin our lives with adoring parents who celebrate every smile or feeble attempt to walk. But as we grow older, that dedicated attention can turn into harsh words and punitive actions.

It's natural for us to believe the beginning is the best. Our world conditions us to believe this. But our heavenly Father is very different. When he gives something, it only gets better with time. He saves the best for last. Returning to our Russian doll analogy, with God, it's like opening a doll to somehow find a bigger and better doll inside it. I know that doesn't make physical or spatial sense, but try to picture it.

## THE WORD

When James writes "the implanted word," he is invoking the great mystery of the gospel. The Greek word he uses for "word" is *logos*. This is the same word that John uses: "In the beginning was the *Word*, and the *Word* was with God, and the *Word* was God" (John 1:1, emphasis added).

I love how *The Passion Translation* brings this out:

In the very beginning the *Living Expression* was already there. And the *Living Expression* was with God, yet fully God. . . .

> And through his creative inspiration
> this *Living Expression* made all things. . . .
> Life came into being because of him,
> for his life is light for all humanity. (vv. 1–4,
> emphasis added)

*Logos* is used by both James and John to convey the totality of the gospel message, God's "powerful self-expression in creation, revelation, and redemption."[1] This self-expression came to us in the form and work of Jesus Christ: the life and light of the world. When we read "implanted word," we must allow our imagination, which is the workshop of faith, to guide us into the awesomeness of what James is writing.

God's plan has always been to give us a new heart and make us partakers of his divine nature through the rebirth of his Spirit (Ezek. 36:27). This is why Jesus told his immediate disciples (and the generations of disciples to come) that it's better for us to be filled with his Spirit than to have him confined to a single body in our dimension: "Nevertheless, I tell you the truth: it is to your advantage that I go away, for if I do not go away, the Helper will not come to you. But if I go, I will send him to you" (John 16:7).

Notice that Jesus had to preface this statement with "I tell you the truth." He knew his words would be hard for his followers to swallow. Put yourself in their shoes. They had lived with Jesus, spending almost every day with him. And often making fools of themselves and needing frequent correction. Yet Jesus tells them it's better for them if he goes away. Why would he say such a thing? Jesus goes on to give the answer: "I still have many things to say to you, but you cannot bear them now. When the Spirit of truth comes, he will guide you into all the truth" (vv. 12–13).

The disciples could not understand the depths of Jesus's message because they had yet to receive his Spirit. Only like can know like. They needed an infilling of God's Spirit, an infilling that, according to Peter in Acts 2, is available to all of God's Saints. In Jesus, the disciples saw the light, but they would also need his life—his Spirit—if they were to become people who could join Christ's cosmic rescue.

Both John and James make it clear that Jesus is the light and life. In him, we see the light. We see how he lived, loved, and died, all of which points to the Father, whom we cannot see. But an example of life isn't good enough. How many of us have been inspired by great examples but have lacked the power to change our lives?

Jesus was and is the light, revealing and giving visual expression to the way. But Jesus didn't die just to give us a good example—he died to raise us into life. Now that we have his Spirit in us, we can experience his life, harmonizing with his Spirit: "I am the light of the world. Whoever follows me will not walk in darkness, but will have the light of life" (John 8:12).

## DEEP DIVE

The blood of the son of God is the ground of our sanctification, but it is the Holy Spirit who . . . destroy[s] the depravity of our hearts.[2]

Let's return to James 1:

But be doers of the word, and not hearers only, deceiving yourselves. . . .

If anyone thinks he is religious and does not bridle his tongue but deceives his heart, this person's religion is worthless. Religion that is pure and undefiled before God the Father is this: to visit orphans and widows in their affliction, and to keep oneself unstained from the world. (vv. 22, 26–27)

There's a good chance you've heard verse 22 paraphrased: "You have to be a doer of the word, not just a hearer." And, yes, this is true. But sadly, people have used this passage and what James writes in his second chapter about works and faith to promote a salvation that comes from only really good behavior. But James is in no way advocating such a paradigm. What he is suggesting is that we dive deeper into salvation's reality and by doing so find a power that is both metaphysical and practical. A power that can save us from hell and breathe vitality into our lives.

Going back to verse 21, we're told the implanted word is "able to save our souls." There's no question that James is writing to believers, so he's not alluding exclusively to an eternal salvation. The word *souls* is used to convey our minds, wills, and emotions. James is telling us that if we receive the implanted word (a spiritual and metaphysical concept), we will experience salvation of the soul (a practical concept that affects the way we live here and now).

Because we are children of God, the enemy has lost the battle for our spirits, so he's waging war on our soul. He doesn't want us to live in peace, joy, and intimacy. The last thing he wants is for our lives to reveal God's life to our world. He wants Christians to relegate their salvation to an abstract concept that doesn't have much bearing on the real and challenging issues we face today. He's terrified of our unpacking the gift of salvation and finding that there are larger Russian dolls inside.

A small view of salvation creates an escapism mentality—we're just trying to get through this life so we can make it to heaven one day. But that mindset doesn't line up with Scripture, and it keeps us from taking action to heal our world *now* by partnering with God's Spirit. James's call to action is greater than moralism or following the rules. James is challenging us to embrace our True Self and reveal God's ways to our world.

When James tells us to be doers of the word and not hearers only, he's reminding us to find our lives in Christ and not in the futility of our own strength. He has just promised us that the gospel message as revealed in and through Christ has been woven into our new nature, our new identity. Peter tells us that we've become partakers of the divine nature (2 Pet. 1:4). John tells us that God's eternal seed, his Spirit, is in us (1 John 3:9). It's not about us making ourselves better people; it's about us laying our opinions of ourselves at the cross so we can experience new creation reality. Sometimes the hardest thing for us to let go of is our opinion of ourselves. But death to the False Self is the only way to find life.

## WHAT DO YOU LOOK LIKE?

> For if anyone is a hearer of the word and not a doer, he is like a man who looks intently at his natural face in a mirror. For he looks at himself and goes away and at once forgets what he was like. But the one who looks into the perfect

law, the law of liberty, and perseveres, being no hearer who forgets but a doer who acts, he will be blessed in his doing. (James 1:23–25)

So what does James mean by all this mirror talk? The mirror is about remembering both who we are and whose we are. Our relationship with the mirror is a matter of identity.*

This passage is crammed with subtleties. In the Greek, there is a qualifying word to "face"—*genesis*—that's difficult to translate without encumbering the text. "This word, which of course exists in English as a transliteration, can have two different meanings here: 'existence' or 'beginning.'"[3] I personally believe James is making the most use of *genesis* by giving it dual purpose. As children of God, we have begun a new existence because of our new identity in Christ. This new existence, the implanted word, the glorious life within, aligns us with the heart and purposes of God and positions us to experience the life we were created for.

When we look in and through the law of liberty, we can see the True Self, the one re-created in Christ. But here's the thing: it's not easy for us to see beyond what's in front of us. Vision is scary; it creates opportunity for disappointment. That's why we often turn from visions of greatness. We're terrified of disappointment or failure. Like Simba in Disney's *The Lion King*, we run away and try to hide who we are, forgetting who our Father is.

---

* In James's time, mirrors weren't made from glass, and they didn't do a great job of reflecting anything. It was common for people to actually forget what they looked like. Mirrors are everywhere today, so it's difficult to fathom the idea of forgetting what we look like.

James is reminding us that our salvation (new identity) is not a by-product of our efforts. It is a gift from our Father, the Author of life. God has created the road—all we need to do is move our feet in the right direction.

God celebrates any attempt at movement, just as a parent rejoices at their child's first step. My wife and I couldn't wait to capture our firstborn's first steps on video. Were those first steps worthy of an Olympic Gold? No. Every movement was shaky. Asher looked like a drunk man trying to pass a sobriety test. But the joy was not in the degree of the accomplishment; rather, it was found in the direction. God is more concerned about our trajectory than our level of accomplishment. There are people who appear to be spiritual giants, but their lives are less healthy than those of spiritual babes because they've stopped moving forward. They've grown complacent and will soon find themselves joining the Pharisees, feeding off their own righteousness.

＋I＋

The law of liberty is the law of the new covenant, the one that is found in the nature and example of Jesus Christ. This is why James tells us to look at this law. It's called the law of liberty because it frees us from the confines of the False Self. Its robustness brings us into the family of God, making us descendants of Abraham and recipients of the promise God gave to Abraham in Genesis 12. It's a law born of the Spirit, and only the Spirit knows the deep things of God. We can understand and receive it in our hearts, but it is infinite by nature and cannot be fit nicely into cognitive confines. We can, however, find signposts for it, markers that move us in the right direction (though we must be careful not to call the signposts the real thing).

When we see ourselves through the law of liberty, we see our new nature re-created in God's likeness. We're invited to look into the perfect law of liberty and see the perfection God has in store for us: "For God has re-created you all over again in his perfect righteousness, and you now belong to him in the realm of true holiness" (Eph. 4:24 TPT).

Jesus is the fulfillment of the Mosaic law. He was able to remove the law's casing and reveal its true form, a form that could only be seen in the person of Jesus and received by the work of his Spirit (Gal. 3:22–29). God's Spirit within us makes it possible for us to live in the freedom and magnanimity of the law of liberty.

The implanted word, unseen within us, grants us the power to make God's love seen in our world. Jesus is God's demonstration of his love for us; Jesus's Spirit within us should create a practical demonstration of God's love for the world.

To not embrace this new identity and its practical outworking is to forget whose we are and where we come from. We have been re-created in Christ. This is now our true image. This is where we must center ourselves.

It's not easy to see ourselves the way God sees us. We have years of teachers, friends, coaches, and parents interjecting their thoughts on who we are. But these people don't have the right to define us, to create our image. Only God does. And when he looks at us, he sees us through the filter of his perfect Son.

## BE TRUE TO YOU

When people encounter this idea of God seeing them through his perfect Son, they often presume their individuality is lost. But nothing could be further from the truth. God sees us as we are and celebrates our individuality. A return to him is not a loss of individuality; it is the return to our True Self. All the layers of sin and destructive genetic proclivities that masquerade as individuality are removed, and we find ourselves clothed in splendor with his light and life flowing through our veins. God celebrates you as a unique expression of his creative power. Receiving his implanted word will not dehumanize you; it will restore you to the life and vitality of God's original design for you. Only he has the right to define you.

—I—

To receive the implanted word and persevere, seeing ourselves the way God sees us, will lead to a life of "doing." When we understand our identity, we will become doers; our lives will become poetry, brilliantly displaying God's nature to our world.

But doing comes after understanding. Can you imagine someone trying to build a home without knowing how to use a hammer, saw wood, or do math? The notion is absurd. Yet so often we try to build our lives in Christ without first unpacking the gift of salvation and discovering what it truly is—a new identity.

I'm sure you've heard people say, "To thine own self be true." The phrase comes from Shakespeare's *Hamlet* but has been popularized by gurus pushing self-help practices. They declare that the secret to happiness is authenticity— a modern form of nihilism. What's humorous is they are both wrong and right. We do need to be true to ourselves, but as we've seen, our True Self lies under layers of generational proclivities, societal folly, and childhood tragedy. James 1 promises that we can see through all that masquerades as us to the brilliant, unique True Self, the one God designed and imagined before our lives ever began.

In *Hamlet*, when Polonius charges Laertes, his son, to be true to himself, he's not encouraging Laertes to follow his ephemeral fancies, wherever they may take him. His famous words come in the midst of a tirade on prudence and loyalty. The big idea is Laertes should be true to himself so others can count on what he says and does. Polonius was reminding his son of who he is so he wouldn't become someone he's not.

That's what James is getting at with the mirror. Every day we have a choice. Either we can see ourselves as God sees us, through the law of liberty, or we can see ourselves through our False Self.

What's amazing about God's gift of salvation is that it comes with everything we need. To say that it doesn't is to say one could fragment and segment the gospel message and the work of the cross. Such a notion is ludicrous. We receive the Spirit of Christ in full. There's nothing more we can do—it's either there or it isn't. We do, however, determine the degree the implanted word reshapes our lives here and now.

God is not going to impose his will on you. In fact, the only thing he won't do for you is kill you. You have to choose to die to your False Self. If God killed the ugly, selfish thing we call "self," then instead of children made in his likeness, he would have robots. Glorious robots, but robots nonetheless. The whole idea behind salvation is that God is turning us into sons and daughters—a transformation that is made possible only by receiving the Spirit of the perfect Son.

## HEART OF FLESH

I've always been fascinated by Ezekiel. How could you not love a wild man who's unafraid to mobilize dry bones? (If you're unfamiliar with the story, read Ezekiel 37.)

Ezekiel was a prophet. Prophets tap into the heart of God and see things as they should be, not as they are. They are agents of change, realigning us to God's purpose and best for our lives. In short, they're disruptive. But isn't that what we need? If we are going to experience something new, things have to change.

Ezekiel saw our day. He saw the time when God's Spirit would come into our lives and make our hearts his home. He knew the implanted word would change everything, so he boldly wrote what God instructed him to:

> I will give you a new heart, and a new spirit I will put within you. And I will remove the heart of stone from your flesh and give you a heart of flesh. And I will put my Spirit within you, and cause you to walk in my statutes and be careful to obey my rules. (36:26–27)

This prophecy was fulfilled through Jesus's life and death. God has done what we could never do. He has given us a heart of flesh. There's new blood flowing through our veins. Our spiritual DNA has been recrafted by God's eternal seed (1 John 3:9). This is why we can now become doers of the Word and not hearers only.

## THE GRACE BLOCKER

Mirrors can be tricky things. They are supposed to reflect what is there, so we view them as a type of truth teller, something we can count on. But the truth is they are easily compromised.

When the Hubble Space Telescope launched in 1990, operators soon discovered a defect in the mirror that affected the clarity of the telescope's early images. The defect was eventually diagnosed. The problem was the result of a miscalibration. How significant was the mistake? Less than 1/50th of a human hair. That tiny deviation caused significant distortion and kept Hubble from seeing the stars.[4]

In a similar way, there's a nasty little something that keeps us from seeing our new life in Christ.

✦I✦

Did you know there is a way to keep the Spirit of grace from operating in your life? I've heard people say that nothing can separate us from the grace of God, but that is simply not true. Romans 8:35–39 states that nothing can separate us from God's love, but multiple Scripture passages make it clear that there is a grace blocker.

[Scripture] says, "God opposes the proud but gives grace to the humble." (James 4:6)

Clothe yourselves, all of you, with humility toward one another, for "God opposes the proud but gives grace to the humble." (1 Pet. 5:5)

In other words, God gives grace to the humble, and he opposes the proud by withholding his grace.

Pride is the grace blocker. Pride distorts the mirror of understanding.

So what is pride? Pride is when we elevate our opinion over God's. It's when we put more stock in humans than God, worshiping the creation rather than the Creator. Pride is to deny who God has re-created us to be. It is to deny him.

God will not play second fiddle in your life. Either he has the final say or he doesn't. And he will not allow the power of his grace to feed a destructive view of yourself. Pride takes on many different forms: insecurity, doubt, and arrogance, just to name a few. But all these have the same root—a distorted view of your identity in Christ and a low view of God.

Could it be that we don't know who we are in Christ because we've rejected God's true form?

Could it be that we've made a god in our own image instead of allowing God to transform us into his?

We're going to spend the next couple of chapters exploring these questions.

# TO FEAR OR
# NOT TO FEAR?

*The low view of God entertained almost universally
among Christians is the cause of a hundred lesser evils
everywhere among us. . . . The decline of the knowledge
of the holy has brought on our troubles. A rediscovery
of the majesty of God will go a long way
toward curing them.* —A. W. Tozer

I tend to revisit A. W. Tozer's book *A Knowledge of the
Holy* whenever I find myself thinking small thoughts
about God. It's easy to lose sight of who God is. He
is unlike anything we've ever seen or known. How
can we comprehend a God who spans the universe with his
fingers and weighs the seven seas in his hand? (Isa. 40:12).

I agree with Tozer that a low view of God is the cause
of "a hundred lesser evils," but I actually think he's under-
stating the truth. A low view of God isn't the cause of just
a hundred lesser evils—it's the cause of *every* lesser evil in
our world. A low view of God has always been humanity's
undoing.

A big God is a scary thing. In many ways, religion has
spent more time reducing God to systems and formulas than

connecting people to the One who is life beyond measure. In our attempts to be systematic, we've systematically removed the wonder and power of what it means to be the people of God. In our efforts to make God "accessible," we've turned him into a subject of our creation—governed by our rules and expectations.

God created us in his image, and now we return the favor.

We don't want to mess around with a God who is *other* than us. We want a God who is like us. A God who can be controlled by us. We're terrified of a God who can reconcile judgment and mercy, anger and kindness, love and hate, grace and holiness. We want a one-dimensional God. But the God of Scripture is anything but one-dimensional. He is so *other* than us that we can't even grasp his name: I AM, YHWH, the self-sufficient One. The largeness of such a name is terrifying—an assault on our small thinking.

What we can define, we can confine. And in our efforts to define God—for utility's sake—we have confined his expression to the extent of our current being. But we cannot attempt to neuter God and still expect to find life. It just won't happen. If we're going to find life, we'll have to first rediscover its Maker in all his otherness.

It seems humanity's expressed mission does not require a big God—it requires a tame one. It requires pithy answers and powerless platitudes. It requires ease, comfort, and predictability. It requires a theology and a Christology that we can master and control. And as we've lost sight of who God is, we've lost sight of who he's created us to be and what he's called us to do.

## UNAFRAID TO FEAR

There is an evil (personified in Satan) that keeps us from seeing the beauty of life. It makes our lives small, shadows of what we know they could and should be. This evil—our low view of God—cannot be wished away. It must be acknowledged. It must be confronted. It must be overcome. And the only way to overcome it is to dive into fear.

We must become unafraid to fear God.

You might be thinking, *Wait a second, . . . didn't you point out earlier that "do not fear" is the most repeated command in Scripture? Why are you now telling me I must dive into fear? That doesn't make any sense! And isn't God love, the love that casts out fear?*

Fair point. That does seem confusing. Let's find some clarity in 1 John 4:18, the famous verse about perfect love casting out fear: "There is no fear in love, but perfect love casts out fear. For fear has to do with punishment, and whoever fears has not been perfected in love."

Earlier in this letter, John also writes, "God is love" (v. 8). There it is. Perfect Love—God personified—casts out all fear. In light of this, how can we, as children of God, be encouraged to fear the One who is Love?

If we take a closer look at John's words, we'll notice necessary context. And as we all know, context is king.

When John writes "fear has to do with punishment, and whoever fears has not been perfected in love," he's describing a fear oriented in self-preservation—more specifically, the preservation of the False Self. When we are living in Christ, embracing the fullness of our new identity, we can and should jettison this fear. It has no place in our lives.

As we are perfected in love by the Spirit of the fear-of-the-Lord (one of the names given to God's Spirit[1]), we find ourselves wrapped in God's love, unafraid of what may happen to us. Though we know Scripture speaks of a judgment of the righteous, our confidence is found in our Father's mercy and grace. Our confidence is found in his ability to make something good from our lives. We are confident in the life that comes from him.

This is why John later writes:

> God gave us eternal life, and this life is in his Son. Whoever has the Son has life; whoever does not have the Son of God does not have life. I write these things to you who believe in the name of the Son of God, that you may know that you have eternal life. (1 John 5:11–13)

Notice the tense used here: "God *gave* us eternal life." *Gave* is past tense. Long before you were born, Jesus did what we could never do. Because of his death and resurrection, eternal life is ours. This new life in Christ invades this present age—delivering us from its powers—and shapes the promised age to come. "[Jesus] gave himself for our sins," Paul writes, "to deliver us from the present evil age" (Gal. 1:4).

When the apostle John writes "perfect love casts out fear," he is not referring to all types of fear. He's specifically addressing an unhealthy fear that stems from a False Self focus. John's letter reveals that the opposite of this kind of fear is to lose our lives in perfect love. Perfect love is embracing the implanted word, a new life in Christ, so we can extend God's love and life into our world. "By this we know love, that he laid down his life for us, and we ought to lay down our lives. . . . Let us not love in word or talk but in deed and in truth" (1 John 3:16).

This freedom from fear is found only in the death of the False Self. Dead people don't fear anything. Would a dead person scream if you threw him off a cliff? Does a corpse struggle with concerns about what other people might think of her? To die to the False Self is to be free from the tyranny of small living. It is to awaken, by the Spirit, to God's original design for humanity. It is to become truly human, in the likeness of perfect Love.

There is a fear that keeps us from embracing our freedom in Christ and loving others. That's the fear John is unpacking in his letter. This type of fear is not of God and can be eradicated from our lives only through partnership with the Spirit of Christ.

The problem is we've been taught that all fear is bad. But this simply isn't true. It's foolish to be scared of a rubber snake, but there's nothing wrong with avoiding venomous snakes that kill over ninety thousand people each year.[2]

Scripture—both the New and the Old Testament—records many promises that come with godly fear. Here's just a sampling: God's presence (Ps. 25:14), honor (Prov. 22:4), abundance (Ps. 128:1–2), prolonged life (Prov. 10:27), peace (19:23), protection (14:26). Scripture also makes it clear that godly fear is the beginning of wisdom (Ps. 111:10; Prov. 1:7; 9:10). This wisdom reshapes our lives and world by the power of the cross. This wisdom defines love, truth, justice, and mercy in objective terms, giving them the power to supersede culture's ever-changing definitions. This godly fear causes us to run toward God, not away from him. It causes us to run from our False Self, finding renewed life in Christ. It could be said that with godly fear comes the wisdom (or blueprint) for higher living.

It is in God's presence that we experience the highest consciousness of living (Ps. 16:11), and godly fear can grow only in God's presence because it's developed and formed in our intimacy with him.

As we spend time with God, exploring his depths, we find ourselves overcome by the One who is truly other. In God, we find *the* something that's been missing—*the* thing we've felt but failed to put words to. We were created to know and be known by God, so we will never find satisfaction apart from intimacy with him. In God, we find what our hearts long for. And in the light of who he is, the cares of this world—the things we incessantly invest our lives in—grow strangely dim.

Our perspective changes.

✦—I—✦

At this point, we have to make a decision. Are we going to let God renew our minds, giving us a new perspective? Or will we simply settle for small living and make God just another tool to get what we think we want?

You were created for more, so you will never be satisfied with what you've known. Don't silence that inner voice that tells you there's more. God is the infinite subject. You will need both courage and fear to explore the depths of life and find its most wonderful treasures.

Deep calls to deep.


## FEAR GOD

In Exodus 20:20, Moses says to the Israelites, "Do not fear, for God has come to test you, that the fear of him may be before you, that you may not sin." It seems as if Moses is talking out of both sides of his mouth. He's basically saying, "Do not fear, God's come to see if you fear him."

In all its ambiguity, this verse provides clarity as to why we should move beyond our one-dimensional view of fear. As we're starting to see, there's a big difference between *being afraid of God* and *fearing him*.

In Exodus 20, God was coming to meet with his people. His goal in delivering them from Egypt was not to bring them to the promised land. His goal was to bring Israel to himself. Relationship was his aim. He split the Red Sea for intimacy. But Israel spurned God's advances. They didn't want a relationship; they wanted a contract—a list of dos and don'ts that would give them the life they wanted. They didn't realize that in God's presence is the highest consciousness of living. It was easier for them to stick with what was familiar, what was easy. Some of them even wanted to return to the whips and chains of Egypt—and a hundred lesser evils.

In splendor, God—the consuming fire—had come to make them whole, purging anything that did not offer life. But in self-preserving terror, Israel ran from the wholeness of relationship and found themselves in the arms of religion—a ruthless taskmaster. God's original plan was for Israel to be a nation of priests, but now he would have to create a priestly sect,[3] distancing himself from the people he loved. In his goodness, he gave them rules and guidelines, things that would help them enjoy what life they could, things that could offer a taste of what he meant for them. But since they ran from the fire of his presence, he could not make them whole.

God's fire and judgment are unleashed on the selfishness that steals our vitality. Israel had been infected by Egypt's ways. They had learned a way of living that had to be unlearned. So God couldn't take them to the promised land (the good life) without first bringing them to the Promiser (the source of life).

## THE PROMISER

For hundreds of years, Israel prayed to be delivered from Egyptian slavery. When the great exodus finally came, it was an event without rival—a story so amazing that we still make movies to tell its splendor. (Cue *The Prince of Egypt*.)

God delivered his people so they could experience the true end and scope of life, which is him. But Israel's infatuation with their deliverance had become an idol. They had certain ideas of what deliverance and life should look like, so they became petulant when God's ways didn't match their own. They wanted deliverance without the Deliverer, the promised land without the Promiser. They were afraid of God, but they didn't fear God, so they ran from his glory.

As my dad says, "The fear-of-the-Lord isn't to be afraid of God; it's to be afraid of being away from God." To fear God is to stay in his presence, seeking to know ourselves through our Creator's eyes. To fear God is to find ourselves overcome by the One who is perfect in every sense—perfect in measures and ways we don't even know exist.

To fear God is to know the beauty of Life.

Moses was scared to be away from God because in God he had seen something that was unlike anything he had ever seen or known. In God, he saw something and someone who was truly other. He knew there was no true life away from God. This is why Moses was drawn to God. Moses feared him. Moses yielded his life to God's truths. He found God on the mountain, and while he was lost in God's presence for forty days and nights, Israel, the people who were afraid of God and only wanted rules to follow, were in the valley "breaking the rules" and degrading themselves (Exod. 32). Their choices were evidence that they had never known the mountainous air of higher living.

In frustration with his people, God suggested that Moses lead Israel to the promised land without him. To sweeten the deal, he would send a warring angel to drive out Israel's enemies. If this offer had been extended to the masses, there would have been deafening chants of "Angel!" But listen to how Moses responded to God's offer: "If your presence will not go with me, do not bring us up from here" (33:15).

Moses had learned there wasn't much outside of God's presence. Israel had seen God's power, but Moses was learning God's ways. Israel wanted results; Moses longed for relationship.

I have no doubt Moses was excited to possess the promised land, but he was much more interested in being possessed by the Promiser. Moses knew that lands come and go. He knew there were days of victory and defeat ahead. He knew that life isn't confined to a particular place in time—it's about being connected to the One who transcends time.

Sadly, a whole generation of Israelites missed out on the good life (the promised land). When their deliverance came, it became plain their imprisonment was internal. A change in scenery wouldn't change anything. In fact, the promised land would have only made it harder for them to recognize their condition. God, in his mercy, extended their time in the desert, offering a chance at true freedom.

Our good Father will not deliver us from trouble when he knows that trouble will deliver us from ourselves.[4]

## LACK IN ABUNDANCE

In America, we live in a land of promise. A land flowing with milk and honey. There's abundance everywhere. It's estimated we throw away 160 billion dollars' worth of produce every twelve months.[5] That's enough produce to feed entire countries for a year.

We're surrounded by beauty and abundance. Life is full of good gifts. But it's easy for us to lose sight of the Giver in the gifts. These gifts are amazing and add color to our lives, but they do not create life.

> Modern civilization has raised the material level of millions of people beyond the expectations of the past, [but] has it succeeded in making people happier? To judge by the bulk of modern literature, we would have to answer "No"; and in some respects, we might even have to say it has accomplished the reverse.[6]

Yet how often do we find a measure of comfort or happiness in believing the "next thing" will give us what we're lacking? The next job, that other marriage, the next vacation, that other device, the next opportunity, that other house, the next promotion—the list has no end. Finding worth and stability in these things creates a perversion of hope. This is the kind of hope that makes the heart sick. It feels like hope, but it lacks substance.

Our advances in science, medicine, and technology are incredible. We live in a comfort and security that are unprecedented. We know more about our anatomy and biochemistry than ever before. Yet depression and suicide are on the rise. Even Jungian psychologist James Hillman titled one of his books *We've Had a Hundred Years of Psychotherapy—And the World's Getting Worse.*\*

There is a plethora of options to distract us from the pain and discomfort that come with underliving. Many of

---

\* For the record, I do think there is such a thing as healthy counseling, especially if the counselor directs the patient toward true health and doesn't placate symptoms to merely create clinical dependency.

us can be found scrolling through our feed while we brush our teeth or sit at red lights. We don't create space for deep thought. We don't make room to know the condition of our souls.

How can we know the otherness of God when we're afraid of being still? As T. S. Eliot wrote:

> Knowledge of speech, but not of silence
> Knowledge of words, and ignorance of the
>     Word. . . .
> Where is the Life we have lost in living?[7]

Many thought leaders have recognized our addiction to incessant activity and are now recommending meditation and contemplation. My hope is that such practices will reduce the noise and awaken the senses. If we quiet ourselves, we'll find there are rudimentary questions (and answers) on belonging, purpose, and identity that must be acknowledged if we are going to enjoy the higher living God has for us.

I believe there is a great awakening coming. People are going to rise from their stupor and realize they've been medicated for too long.

In many ways, our technology-driven world is speeding up the iterations of human pursuit, creating more disappointments in less time. We've gone from using a single hook to fish the seas of meaning to employing giant nets. We're catching more fish than ever before. The problem is none of these fish is the one we're looking for. People are frustrated because it would seem that with the number of fish we're pulling in, we should be catching the right one.

◆I◆

Despite our foolish self-absorption, God remains patient with us. As a parent, sometimes I have a hard time not giving my kids the answers they seek. When I was teaching my daughter Sophia to read, it took everything in me not to read the word for her. She'd struggle for what felt like minutes (even though it was probably only a few seconds). I'd see her anguish and want to reach out and give her the right word. But I knew my intervention would only inhibit real growth. Yes, with my help she'd finish the book faster—but she'd likely struggle just as much the next time she read it.

Peter writes that God is patient because he doesn't want any of us to perish (2 Pet. 3:9). As a good father, he wants to make us whole. I've heard human history described as a divine agony, God desiring to give his life to us.[8] Aren't you amazed by his patience? Despite the fact we faithfully reject him, he faithfully offers his life to us.

But God will not give us life on our terms. And for that reason, true life will end up looking different than we expect.

## THE FIRE OF GOD

God is a consuming fire. Anything that is not of him will be exposed and eliminated. God doesn't judge us to get rid of us. He judges us to get rid of the things that would get rid of us.

God's fire is unlike earthly fire in this sense: the closer you get to it, the less it burns. Yes, those initial steps are excruciating and produce a hideous aroma. But isn't that what's to be expected? Something is dying, and death is dreadful and repugnant. But as we journey toward the glory that is God, the pain turns into promise. A promise that he will not abandon us. A promise that he *will* love us unto wholeness and loveliness, no matter what it costs him.

God's goodness, grace, and mercy aid our death to self. God never loses sight of our True Self. He infuses our journey of liberation with faith, hope, and love. His faith offers us the power to go beyond the confines of our fallen humanity. His hope offers us a picture to run toward. And his love is forever working with us, opening our eyes to the wonders of life.

This is our God. There is no one like him.

## ISAIAH'S VISION

In the year that King Uzziah died I saw the Lord sitting upon a throne, high and lifted up; and the train of his robe filled the temple. Above him stood the seraphim. Each had six wings: with two he covered his face, and with two he covered his feet, and with two he flew. And one called to another and said:

> "Holy, holy, holy is the LORD of hosts;
> The whole earth is full of his glory!"

And the foundations of the thresholds shook at the voice of him who called, and the house was filled with smoke. And I said: "Woe is me! For I am lost; for I am a man of unclean lips, and I dwell in the midst of a people of unclean lips; for my eyes have seen the King, the LORD of hosts!"

Then one of the seraphim flew to me, having in his hand a burning coal that he had taken with tongs from the altar. And he touched my mouth and said: "Behold, this has touched your lips; your guilt is taken away, and your sin atoned for."

And I heard the voice of the Lord saying, "Whom shall I send, and who will go for us?" Then I said, "Here I am! Send me." (Isa. 6:1–8)

The sixth chapter of Isaiah gives me chills. It's one of the few (nearly) unbridled accounts of God. In this scene, Isaiah, a prophet and holy man, finds himself in God's presence, overtaken by the wonder of YHWH—the self-sufficient One.

Most scholars believe Isaiah experienced a heavenly vision, a vision that escaped the bounds of Isaiah's vocabulary and conception. In his futility, Isaiah resorted to obscure language. Metaphorical statements such as "the train of his robe filled the temple" (whatever that means) are necessary because he's struggling to put words to what he saw.

Ezekiel had a similar encounter with the Holy One (Ezek. 1). His description has even more metaphors and hedging qualifiers. In fact, Ezekiel sounds like a middle schooler trying to describe a person: "You know, he's kind of like, that person, you know, kind of, like, you know." But instead of "You knows," "kind ofs," and "likes," Ezekiel uses "like," "the likeness of," "their appearance was like," "like the appearance of," and "the appearance of the likeness of the glory."

I'm not picking on middle schoolers. Our world disdains the notion of objectivity, so hedging qualifiers and modifiers are ubiquitous in speech (and not just among teenagers).

I'm merely making the point that Ezekiel and Isaiah both struggled to express what they were seeing.

As humans, we learn through association. We build on prior knowledge to learn new things. Everything we understand was first understood by understanding something else. (How's that for a confusing sentence?)

If you look at our greatest inventions, you can trace their evolution back to rudimentary ideas and basic inventions. All of our complex reasoning and innovation is merely a new combination of old ideas. As created beings, we can manipulate creation, but only God has the power to create something truly new.

God belongs to a different category, one that is completely his own. "That is why we can't expect to mount a ladder of [logic] from our world and end up in his, any more than we might expect to mount a ladder of moral achievement and end up making ourselves good enough to stand in his presence."[9]

## HOLY, HOLY, HOLY

Both Ezekiel and Isaiah found themselves in the presence of something and someone that was entirely *other*.

In their accounts of God, both men wrote of bizarre creatures that were worth mentioning. There's a lot of speculation about what these creatures actually are, but my goal isn't to convince you of what they are. I just want to look at what they're doing.

These creatures are also found in the book of Revelation. Night and day, they cry, "Holy, holy, holy" (4:8).

It's important to note that the threefold "holy" is not an attempt to create a melody. Rather, in the Hebrew language, the repetition of a word is a way of expressing a superlative idea.[10] The key word here is *superlative*, which conveys the highest degree of quality. In these instances, the triple cry is the highest form of elevation. It is the degree of holy that solely belongs to God, a holiness that is found and experienced in God's dimension, or the third heaven.[11] It would be more appropriate to imagine these creatures declaring or announcing God's holiness as opposed to singing about it.

The creatures are not declaring love, love, love. Is God love? Yes, absolutely. But love is not God's superlative quality. God's holiness is what makes his love transcendent. The creatures are reacting to the wonder of God's otherness. In its purest form, this is what *holy* or *holiness* means—there is no one like God; he is set apart, entirely *other*.[12] That's why God's holiness is the foundation of his other transcendent qualities, including love. Listen to what the creatures declare after crying holy:

> The whole earth is full of his glory. (Isa. 6:3)

> Who was and is and is to come! (Rev. 4:8)

Both of these expressions of awe offer insight into what the creatures are beholding. In Isaiah's account, the creatures are declaring the expansive reach of God's wonder and majesty. Nothing is off limits to him. In John's account in Revelation, the creatures are celebrating God's eternal nature—something that makes him completely *other* than his creation. They are also, in a sense, prophesying future events when a greater measure of God's majesty will be revealed to our world, reshaping our lives and completing our metamorphosis as the people of God, the people of the One who is other.

The Hebrew word for *holy* in Isaiah 6 is *qadosh*. This word is nearly impossible to define because we don't have language that is robust enough to capture God's otherness. The best attempts to define this word include perfect in goodness and righteousness, set apart, sacred, and consecrated. Unfortunately, none of these words do God's holiness—his *qadosh*—justice, and this disconnect has caused us to create our own idea of holiness, an idea that is synonymous with moral goodness.

The problem with that is we cannot measure God's moral goodness. His ways are higher than our ways (Rom. 11:33–36). But we can stand in awe of his otherness (1 Cor. 2), and when we gaze upon his true form in and by the Spirit (2 Cor. 3:16–18), we become like him, partaking of his divine nature (2 Pet. 1:3–4). As we discover God's holiness, we become like him. We find our otherness, the new creation life in Christ.

*Holy* and *holiness* do convey a form of morality, but any expression of that form is subsequent to and built upon the truth of God's otherness (and our otherness in Christ). Another definition of *Saint* (*hagios*) is "holy one,"[13] or people of God's otherness. We are people who have been infused by God's nature and share a form of his likeness.

This otherness is known only through faith—a faith that expresses itself in surrender. The journey of knowing God invites us to confront darkness and death. Darkness because we step into the unknown. Death because we must die to the Old Self and cast aside our vapid notions of life, love, holiness, and wholeness. But as we journey in, darkness yields to light, and death morphs into new life—the only kind of life worth living.

## LOST FOR WORDS

Let's return to Isaiah's interaction with God: "Woe is me! For I am lost; for I am a man of unclean lips, and I dwell in the midst of a people of unclean lips; for my eyes have seen the King, the LORD of hosts!" (Isa. 6:5).

Just a chapter earlier, Isaiah was calling out the greedy, the drunkards, the evildoers, and so on. But now he's crying, "Woe is me! For I am lost; for I am a man of *unclean lips*, and I dwell in the midst of a people with *unclean lips*" (emphasis added).

Something must have changed.

The obvious and immediate explanation for Isaiah's sudden change of heart was his awareness of his moral inferiority in the presence of God's purity. But hopefully you're starting to see there's more to the story. It's not that Isaiah's cry was a response to seeing God abstain from doing bad things. Rather, Isaiah found himself lost in the One who has no end and no beginning.

The phrase "for I am lost" could be better translated "I must be silent."[14] In truth, Isaiah was both lost and at a loss for words. How could Isaiah, a mere mortal—confined to time, space, and matter—give utterance to something beyond the grasp of any point of reference? How could he find words to describe the One who is truly other? This was the hopelessness that Isaiah, a prophet of God, felt in that moment.

As a prophet, Isaiah was expected to be a mouthpiece for God. He was expected to lead the people back to the heart of truth. But now that Isaiah has seen God, he is crying, "Woe is me!" In that moment, everything Isaiah knew became suspect, especially his calling and identity. He thought he was a man of God, but now he's not so sure. He thought he was God's mouthpiece, but now that seems impossible.

Then God did what only he can do. His holy love compelled him to cross the great divide, one that could never be traversed by mere words and logic: "Then one of the seraphim flew to me, having in his hand a burning coal that he had taken with tongs from the altar. And he touched my mouth and said: 'Behold, this has touched your lips; your guilt is taken away, and your sin atoned for'" (vv. 6–7).

Isaiah did have a profound awareness of his sins and failings. But the bigger picture here is Isaiah's awareness of his inability to articulate the glory and wonder before him. In other words, he had an undeniable revelation of God's otherness, but he knew there weren't words to capture the One who is simply I AM.

It's very important to note that the burning coal from the presence of God—the highest state of consciousness and understanding—was placed on Isaiah's mouth. God was responding to Isaiah's cry of "I must be silent." Isaiah humbled himself in the presence of God, and in return

God gave him the capacity to understand and speak. Isaiah had done nothing to receive such a gift. This gift from the presence of God was a foretaste of the Messiah's future accomplishment, when Christ would secure our forgiveness, purification, atonement, and new life in his Spirit.

After Isaiah received this gift of knowing, he volunteered to be God's messenger. The man who cried "Woe is me!" has been infused with Life. The man who said "I must be silent" is brimming over with words. Isaiah went on to pen a masterpiece, a book that has been revered for millennia, all because of an encounter with God's otherness.

When Isaiah saw God, everything changed.

## SHUDDER

As I mentioned before, the prophet Ezekiel had a similar encounter. He too found himself hopelessly overwhelmed by God's otherness. Like Isaiah, Ezekiel was a prophet, a holy man. But after experiencing a vision of heaven (God's dimension), he fell on his face in worship and terror. His mind simply could not process what his eyes were seeing. But then God said, "Stand on your feet, and I will speak with you" (Ezek. 2:1). And, once again, God did what only he can do. He crossed the eternal divide by becoming the bridge: "And as [God] spoke to me, the Spirit entered into me and set me on my feet, and I heard him speaking to me" (v. 2).

God's Spirit, the Spirit that hovered over the waters and created life in the beginning (and sustains life today), is the agent of new creation. God's Spirit entered Ezekiel and gave him the capacity to articulate and follow his ways. God's otherness invaded Ezekiel, and he became a new man. Ezekiel found himself filled with courage and confidence, overflowing with words that still mystify and inspire us today.

◆I◆

St. Augustine wrote, "What is that which gleams through me and smites my heart without wounding it? I am both a-shudder and a-glow. A-shudder, in so far as I am unlike it, a-glow in so far as I am like it."[15] When we shudder in God's presence, we'll glow in our world. And that's exactly what happened to Ezekiel and Isaiah.

God has made a way for us to know him deeply and intimately. But this cannot happen until we first fear him, standing in awe of his holiness, love, and beauty—our False Self overcome by his otherness. "When accepted as unknown," wrote H. A. Williams, "the Unknown becomes paradoxically well-known."[16]

God's distance—his ways being so much higher than ours—somehow brings him close to us. The God who can span the universe with his hands knows the subtleties of the heart. Your heart, to be more specific. Unlike with our earthly giants of culture, God's grandeur makes him more accessible. He doesn't lose touch with reality because reality flows through him. He can't forget about you because you are in him, moving, being, and existing in his breath.

We are invited to "serve the LORD with fear, and rejoice with trembling" (Ps. 2:11). Rejoicing abounds in the presence of the One who makes us tremble to our core. When we shudder in the presence of God, the One who is simply I AM WHO I AM, we shake off what is not us. There's a metamorphic, and at times violent, return to our True Self, our original self. We are re-created in godly fear, and in his awesome presence, we find our true humanity, we find life.

In the light of God's greatness, our False Self loses its luster, and we find that the life we've been desperate to hold on to is merely a mirage. But we cannot step into the otherness God has for us if we refuse to embrace his otherness. He must be regarded as holy by those who would come near him. That's why we, the Saints, must worship God with astonishment. After all, "a God comprehended is no God."[17]

> Oh, fear the LORD, you his saints,
>     for those who fear him have no lack! (Ps. 34:9)

The fear-of-the-Lord is an invitation to intimacy and life beyond anything we have ever known. The question is, Will we be *intimate* with this God, or will we run from the arms of Life?

We need to return to a childlike sense of wonder. We've made all of this too safe, too familiar. And in doing so, we've made our lives small.

## GOD'S FINGERS

It was bedtime in the Bevere house—which means my kids secretly brainstorm questions that are sure to add another

twenty minutes or so to their wake time. But on this particular night, it wasn't a question that stimulated our noc-
turnal dialogue. It was a comment.

Asher, who was seven at the time, remarked, "Dad, I'd
like to visit the places where you can still see God's fingerprints. Could you take me to see those places?"

At first, I didn't know how to respond. Truth be told,
I didn't really know what he was talking about. "Asher,"
I replied, "what do you mean by God's fingerprints?"

Without hesitation, Asher rejoined, "You know, Dad,
the holes in the earth that were made when God first spun
the earth into motion. I want to see those holes . . . the
ones created by his fingers gripping the earth."

When I look at your heavens, the work of your fingers . . .
(Ps. 8:3)

I almost told Asher it didn't work like that. I almost gave
him truncated theory, science, and religion.

But God's Spirit stopped me. Asher's understanding of
the earth's formation was probably closer to the truth than
science can take us. The Spirit did, after all, hover over the
waters, like a mother over her young. There's tenderness
in the hovering. Matter—water, air, dust—is precious to
God. Clearly, he likes to get his hands dirty.

After months of reflecting on Asher's statement, I'm convinced that God's fingerprints are all around us. We live in
their shadows, do business in their bluffs, and drive along
their corridors. The beauty of nature invites us to be intimate
with the Creator.

Paul's summation is brilliant: "Since we have these promises [of intimacy with God], beloved, let us cleanse ourselves from every defilement of body and spirit, bringing holiness to completion in the fear of God" (2 Cor. 7:1). God's holiness—the otherness that our hearts crave—becomes alive in us as we intimately fear God. Run to the arms of your Father. Ask for eyes to see him as he is. The Lover of your soul stands at your door and knocks. When you invite him in, he will fill your soul with the eternal. He will give you the only things worth having. Become rich in love, become rich in wisdom and grace, become rich in him. And from your place of abundance, give everything you have, here and now, to those who have yet to know how lovely they are.

# INTO FEAR

*For you formed my inward parts;*
*you knitted me together in my mother's womb.*
*I praise you, for I am fearfully and wonderfully made.*
*Wonderful are your works; my soul knows it very well.*

*—Psalm 139:13–14*

Does it now seem strange that the word *fear-fully* is used in Psalm 139:14? I love how the inspired author uses *fear* when describing the intimate process of creation.

Verse 14 may be better translated "for I am awesomely and fearfully [*yare*] set apart [*palah*]" (my translation). It's interesting that the psalmist also writes, "My soul knows it very well." Deep down, we know we were created for more. And this scares us. After all, what exactly is that more? But the psalmist tells us not to fear our otherness— the thing that sets us apart. It's a gift from God. It's a gift from his otherness.

Yet we often deny that we are fearfully and wonderfully made because that would require too much of us. We turn this fact into a slave master instead of allowing it to be our liberator. It enslaves us because we don't have eyes to see how God sees us. But not having eyes to see won't change who we are any more than blindness can change the color of our skin. In the same way, we cannot deny our True Self out of existence, whether we "see" it or not. It is, after all, the only real self.

You are fearfully and wonderfully made. Period.

In that knowledge comes the confidence and the humility that propel us into an awakening of God's greatness within us. God deals in paradoxes—so though it may seem as if confidence and humility live on opposite poles, wholeness requires us to bring them both to the center of our being, refusing to reduce or eliminate either quality. At this intersection of confidence and humility, we find vulnerability.

God becoming man was the ultimate act of vulnerability. He didn't just win our hearts through a metaphysical battle that was beyond the reach of human comprehension. He came to earth as one of us. He was betrayed, abandoned, tempted, and, ultimately, he tasted death. He bled our blood, sweat our sweat, cried our tears, walked our roads. Jesus became intimate with our joy and pain, holding back nothing so that we could have everything.

Notice that the psalmist goes on to write, "Wonderful are your works." God's creation is full of wonder, and humanity is the apex of his design. We are the ones made in his image. He has given us everything—life and love in their fullness.

The psalmist cannot proclaim God's brilliance and deny his own intrinsic value and beauty at the same time, and neither can we. To deny our value is to deny God's creative power. It is to deny his glory. You might think this sounds humanistic, but I'd argue that no other person has seen so much potential in humanity. Jesus knows our inner workings—he participated in giving us life. He knows who we are and what we are capable of.

We are fearfully and wonderfully made because we were made for intimacy. We were made for God's presence. We were made in his love. Our depths and layers are evidence of his handiwork. With King David we cry, "Who am I that you are mindful of me?" (Ps. 8:4). And God responds, "You are everything to me. After all, I intimately formed you in your mother's womb. Now take the plunge into my love and know life without measure" (my paraphrase).

## INTIMACY

When I was a kid, *intimacy* was the word my parents used when they were uncomfortable saying *sex*. For the longest time, sex and intimacy felt synonymous to me. But intimacy is obviously more than sex and reaches beyond marital relations. *Merriam-Webster* defines *intimate* as "belonging to or characterizing one's deepest nature."[1]

Did you catch that? "One's deepest nature." Intimacy becomes a mirror, reflecting the hidden parts of our being. True intimacy will dismantle our facades, leaving us exposed, warts and all.

There's nothing scarier than intimacy—that's probably why we call it "scary close." Some even believe that our word *intimacy* evolved from the Latin *in timor*, or "into fear."

Intimacy bypasses our barriers. It soars beyond the walls of superficiality and lands on the plains of authenticity and vulnerability. It calls for us to live beyond ourselves, going deeper to give more. Without it, we cannot love and be loved. Without intimacy, we cannot become our True Self.

That's why it's terrifyingly wonderful.

True intimacy offers no place for self-preservation, which, as we saw in the previous chapter, is the root of fear. God's design for intimacy requires an exchange of selves—a laying down of our lives. We give God our Old Self, and he gives us a New Self infused with his life. This exchange is the antithesis of self-preservation and embodies love at its best.

This exchange is the great dive into fear.

The challenge is we don't have a model for this radical exchange of selves. At one time, marriage was considered sacred because it was the closest thing to such an exchange. Scripture uses the marriage covenant to create a glimpse into God's devotion for us. Now marriages are discarded like last week's garbage, and we are left wondering whether the transcendence of selfless love actually exists.

Tragically, our fear *to love* blinds us to our worthiness *of love*. We relentlessly pursue self-preservation because we don't realize our intrinsic value. We hoard what we do have because it seems small, and we're terrified of other people discovering our smallness. What we have is too "small" to share. This mentality keeps us from enjoying the intimacy that God designed us for—both with him and with others.

But when we dive into fear and become intimate with the One who gave his life for us, losing our apparent smallness in his largeness, we embrace the only One who has the right to set our value. In his intimate embrace, we find the courage to discover and become who he created us to be. And from this place of surrender, we find the perspective to love fearlessly.

## FEAR TO LOVE

When people don't know they're fearfully made, they'll run from deep relationships. It's no surprise fear ruins more relationships than anything else.

My wife, Julianna, was a player before we met, one of those girls who parties hard and dangles boys on strings. Through a strange sequence of events, we met and enjoyed some witty banter. She thought I was cute and different, so she went out with the "Christian boy." Little did she know that I had mad game and would flirt to convert. (Okay, that's not true. I hadn't been on a date in a long time.)

But within one week of our first date, we knew we wanted to get married. At the time, my wife lived in Texas and had made plans to attend a state university. But after a week of knowing me, she decided to look into Bible school.

I was puzzled by her decision. I tried to explain to her that she didn't need to go to Bible school to be a Christian. But she was determined to make the leap and do something she would have scoffed at just a couple of weeks earlier.

When we met, she didn't know much about God or the Bible. I asked her what John 3:16 said, and she couldn't tell me. Her religious illiteracy—something that was very attractive to me—made her feel inadequate and ill-positioned to be in love with the son of a preacher man.

Julianna ended up choosing an intense, legalistic school that basically took over her life. The program was designed to develop a person's mind, body, and spirit. The students would run marathons, climb mountains, do missions, and so on. This program was not for the faint of heart, and many people dropped out of the school.

Upon learning that Juli and I were in love and wanted to get married one day, the leadership of the school decided to remove me from Juli's life. Essentially, they did this by forbidding any communication. We weren't even allowed to write letters. For 275 days, neither of us was allowed to affirm our love for each other. Of course, this didn't stop me from writing her every day. I just wasn't allowed to send the letters. After 275 days, I had over four hundred pages to give to her.

During our time of separation, I had to fight so many fears. Fears that tried to keep me from loving her sacrificially. Fears that tried to convince me that her relationship with God was a farce and that she would soon be flirting with the new guys at school.

But I kept pushing my fears back by running toward them. I kept pouring my heart onto those pages. I would dismantle fears by writing in faith. Every day I reminded Julianna of my love for her and who God was re-creating her to be. I knew she felt unworthy and inadequate, so I filled pages with prophetic declarations about her wisdom and splendor. I'm sure there was some part of me that believed those words could escape their paper prison and travel to Julianna's heart on the wings of true love. You know, *Princess Bride*–type stuff.

I knew that God had called me to love her, so I was going to love her the best I could—even if that love resulted in painful heartbreak. Our time apart forged a selfless love in me. I came to terms with the fact that she could emerge from the program and no longer love me.

But after 275 days, I found myself in the arms of a woman who had profoundly changed yet was still the same, a woman who was capable of loving me more deeply. Julianna had

found herself in the eternal arms of Love, and she was committed to loving me from that place of confidence and surrender.

We got married four months later, and we've now been
married over a decade and have four kids. I'm not going to
say our relationship is perfect, but it's something special.

We both fought fears during our time of separation, and
those fears led to an emptying of ourselves. We learned that
when we empty what is "us," God fills us with something
that is "more us." This is one of the great paradoxes of
being. We still have a lot of room for growth (a whole lot
of room for growth), but we've learned the only way to
love deeply is to take the plunge into intimacy.

## SELF-PRESERVATION

Obviously, intimacy looks different in each of our relationships, but any relationship worth having will require you
to face off with the desire for self-preservation. Sure, there
will be those who will take advantage of your selflessness.
(Just look at Jesus—no one has ever been more exploited
than him.) But there is nothing like the joy and wholeness
that come with true relationships.

Our world tells us we can have intimacy without commitment, but that's simply not true. Artificial intimacy is
relationship without consequence. You cannot know joy
without opening yourself to pain. But even in the pain of
disappointment, we can find the power and the perspective
to know true love.

Who are you scared to love? I can promise you that
what's holding you back from loving that person is a low

view of God. When we realize the depths of God and his love for us—the depths of his commitment and grace—we can jettison the smallness of self-preservation and find ourselves infused with a love, courage, and joy that will astound the people in our world.

Jesus said, "A new commandment I give to you, that you love one another: just as I have loved you, you also are to love one another. By this all people will know that you are my disciples, if you have love for one another" (John 13:34–35). He shared these words just hours before his betrayal and death. He was about to take up his cross, and he needed his disciples to know life could only be found by following in his footsteps. In the years leading up to this, Jesus was gently (and sometimes not so gently) leading them into the waters of new life. But the time had come for him to dive into stronger and deeper currents, revealing a new way of being and birthing a new type of humanity. A humanity pulsing with God's Spirit, love, and grace. A people of his otherness—his Saints—set apart for true holiness.

Because of Jesus's life and death, we too can become the people of God, those who live in the deeper waters of being. But we must take the plunge and lose our lives for love.

## LOVE'S SACRIFICE

There is a selfless love that can only be known in the embrace of Love. This selfless love frees us from our selfishness. Many of us use benevolence to feel better about ourselves or to help us sleep at night. When we do this, we are still holding on to the False Self. We may appear selfless, but we are really self-consumed. It's sobering to know that we can give away everything (even sacrificing our bodies) and still be found without love (1 Cor. 13:3).

The true love described in 1 Corinthians 13 comes from "the inner depths of the heart as an eternal energy." It is an active power that bonds "hearts and lives in secure relationships."[2] Paul uses the Greek word *agape*, which describes the highest form of love—a love that is eternal, emanating from the One who is eternal.

There are people who have died giving their lives for glory, yet they lacked any love for the people they were apparently dying for. Such a love is self- and glory-centric. While it may seem beautiful, admirable, and worth celebrating, at the end of the day, it "gains nothing."

Losing our lives for love doesn't always mean losing our breath. When Jesus says, "Greater love has no one than this, that someone lay down his life for his friends" (John 15:13), he is not merely speaking of losing our mortal lives. We Westerners can hardly relate to the idea of literally dying for someone else.

In John 15, Jesus is speaking prophetically of Calvary, *but* he is also inviting us to partake of this same death (and the same love). This "great love" cannot be known without a form of death. Our God wouldn't dangle great love and not give us the means to experience such love. In Christ, we have the pathway to every truly great thing. But we must learn to follow him and practice the rhythms of grace.

I want you to notice that Jesus says, "Lay down his life for his *friends*" (emphasis added), not *friend*. It's important to note that he is not strictly alluding to a glorious, sacrificial exchange, like what we see in *Guardians of the Galaxy* when Star-Lord gives his breathing mechanism to Gamora, leaving himself breathless and suspended in space. I don't want to belittle the glory of such a sacrifice, but Jesus has something much bigger in mind.

Jesus is ultimately describing a way of life, a way of dying to the False Self that releases the true life within. This new life may require a mortal sacrifice, but we have to be careful not to limit it to such extreme forms. When we do this, we strip dying of its meaning and application in this cushy, Western world. After all, most of us will never have the opportunity to voluntarily give up our breath.

Such an invitation to grab hold of great love is available to all countries, cultures, and generations. It's ultimately found in Christ's invitation to take up our crosses and follow him. It's found in the process of giving our lives away for the people impacted by who we are and what we do—family, friends, coworkers, neighbors, and others.

This is how you will experience great love.

God's love and holiness compelled him to lay down his life. Now we are invited to know the love that emanates from God's holiness—his superlative quality, the quality that makes us like him. God's Spirit has invaded our lives to make us partakers of his otherness. As Saints—his holy ones—we tap into eternal love, and once we've tasted this heavenly gift, nothing else will do.

We cannot hide from who we are as new creations in Christ. If we do, we will be overwhelmed by internal dissonance. After all, what fellowship does light have with darkness? The old is gone and the new has come (2 Cor. 5:17).

Let's choose to lay aside the Old Self and put on the New Self, washing ourselves of the stench of selfishness (Eph. 4:21–24).

## EUSTACE

As you've likely figured out by now, I was raised on C. S. Lewis. Almost every night I dreamed of Narnia (except for when I had nightmares of being the antichrist or going to school naked).

In Lewis's *The Voyage of the Dawn Treader*, we find Eustace Scrubb, a wretchedly selfish boy. The only thing Eustace loves—other than himself—is his collection of inanimate objects.

In one of my favorite scenes, Eustace leaves the rest of the ship's crew with the laborious task of repairing their broken vessel and stumbles upon a cave full of golden treasures. What he doesn't realize is that he is on a strange island and this is a magical cave—one that turns a greedy soul into the form of a dragon, revealing the inward form of self-love. Upon discovering his transformation into a dragon, Eustace is terrified and believes his "friends" will likely use his misshapenness as a reason to leave him on the lonely island. But over the next few days, Eustace is taken aback by his shipmates' response to his desperate plight. They show themselves kind and compassionate, and Eustace begins to see that he's been the dragon all along.

When his perspective changes, Eustace begins using the strength and utility of his dragon form to help his shipmates make their vessel seaworthy again. This, in a very real way, could be seen as expediting his lonely doom. There is no one else on the island, and because of his size, Eustace can't ride in the ship. And his wings can't carry him for long distances, so island hopping isn't an option.

But then Eustace meets Aslan—Lewis's allegorical personification of Jesus, the Lion of Judah. In the dead of night, Aslan invites Eustace to make the journey to a magic pool. Although Eustace is a dragon, he's terrified of the lion. But there's something about Aslan that calls to him, so he follows. When they arrive at the pool, Aslan tells Eustace to scratch off his dragon scales. At first, Eustace is confused, but he soon remembers that reptiles shed layers of skin.

Determined, Eustace tries to scratch off his scales. Three times he steps out of his dragon cloak only to find that he just can't seem to scratch deep enough. He is still a dragon, a sore and smaller dragon but a dragon nonetheless. Once Eustace realizes the hopelessness of his efforts, Aslan steps in and does what Eustace can't. Aslan doesn't just scratch off scales; he tears deep into flesh. The process is painful but, at the same time, invigorating. After a night of tearing, Eustace is thrown into the pool and becomes a boy again—a boy who looks the same as before but who is undoubtedly different.

Eustace's scales of fear and selfishness were exposed and removed. In this whole experience, Eustace dove into the fear. Despite Aslan's terrifying otherness, Eustace chose to follow him to the pool and ultimately allowed the lion's claws to dig deep into him. He welcomed Aslan's embrace—the embrace of the One who's "not a tame lion." After his deep dive, Eustace found himself overcome by a love and a safety that were wildly unknown. And with his salvation came the ability to love.

## THE DEEPEST OF INTIMACIES

When we plunge into the living water, we are overtaken by its power and beauty.

I look at the invitation to fear God as a beckoning to partake in the deepest of intimacy. God is the infinite One. He has no limits. Intimacy with him is to take a dive into measureless otherness. Yet his otherness is somehow vaguely familiar. We are, after all, created in his likeness. It is in him that "we live and move and have our being" (Acts 17:28). But we can explore the depths of his person only by losing ourselves in his Spirit. When we do so, we find what we've been searching for. In Paul's first letter to the church at Corinth, he writes, "[God's] Spirit searches everything, even the depths of God. . . . No one comprehends the thoughts of God except the Spirit of God" (1 Cor. 2:10–11).

Notice that God's Spirit searches everything. Later in the chapter, Paul's point climaxes with this statement: "We have the mind of Christ" (v. 16). In other words, God, by his Spirit, gives us access to the depths of understanding. He's not trying to keep us in the dark. Through Christ, we can experience as much of God as we want. We can ask for a greater longing that drives us into the depths of God. As we let him, God's Spirit will work in us to create the desire and the ability to experience more of true life. "Now we have received not the spirit of the world, but the Spirit who is from God, that we might understand the things freely given us by God" (v. 12).

It's nearly impossible for us to be intimate with a majesty beyond us. That's why we're usually most comfortable being intimate with people like us or dependent on us. On some level, intimacy can happen only between those who possess a form of fraternity. That is why Jesus, the Holy One, became a man. He joined humanity's fraternity; he became like us so we could drink deeply of the divine.

Take a moment to read passages such as John 17, Colossians 1–3, and Romans 1–8. You'll see a familial intimacy that transcends time and space, Creator and creation, life and death. This is the great story of our redemption—the story of our becoming sons and daughters, sharing in God's divine nature.

◆I◆

God designed us for intimacy. Even YHWH, the self-sufficient One, is a triune God who models an intimacy, oneness, and interdependence that exceed our comprehension. In *Mere Christianity*, C. S. Lewis describes it this way: "God is not a static thing . . . but a dynamic, pulsating activity, a life, almost a kind of drama. Almost, if you will not think me irreverent, a kind of dance."[3]

Early saints used the Greek word *perichoresis* to describe the dancelike harmony among the Father, Son, and Spirit. This Greek word originally conveyed the idea of moving around in perfect harmony—distinct participants in perfect step. I love the idea of a divine dance. As members of God's family, we are invited to participate in the dance. In fact, nonparticipation isn't an option. The dance requires us to get lost in its rhythm, to move with its cadence. Our steps may be awkward at first and we may hide on the fringes, but the Spirit will find us where we are and move us toward the heart of the movement: "The one who joins himself to the Lord is mingled into one spirit with him" (1 Cor. 6:17 TPT).

Of course, any attempt to assign words to the mystery of God's triune being and our oneness with God will fall short. Even the dance metaphor has its obvious limitations. That's why some things can only be understood in the heart and not articulated with the mouth. Words can be twisted and misused, and these truths are too precious for such abuse.

It's easy to take a dualistic approach to God. He's either a God of judgment or a God of mercy. A God of love or a consuming fire. These apparent contradictions are our inept attempts to schematize God's otherness. The truth is he is all the above. His mercy and judgment are two sides of the same coin. You cannot have one without the other. His love is the fire that eradicates anything that does not yield to the rhythms of life.

In the face of this otherness, we can bolster our pride and dig our heels into the ground. Or we can welcome humility's grace and explore the depths of truth.

## HALF-TRUTHS

Humility invites us to be okay with God being greater than our intellectual and conceptual prowess. We must learn to live in the tension of being fully known while not yet knowing fully. Humility leads us into the expansive life because it keeps us from stopping at partial truths and leads us to whole truths.

Let me be clear—there's nothing wrong with partial truths. If there were, we'd all be in trouble since our lives are built on partial truths: "For we know in part and we prophesy in part, but when the perfect comes, the partial will pass away" (1 Cor. 13:9–10).

But we can turn partial truths into falsehoods when we call them whole truths. Let me give an example. You could say, "Addison has a son," and that would be a true statement. Perhaps you ran into Asher and me somewhere and can now say—with confidence, I might add—that I have a son. There would be an appropriate measure of assurance that comes with your experience and understanding. After all, you did meet him—I introduced Asher to you as my son.

Let's take this a step further. It would be foolish, when asked by someone if I have a son, for you to answer, "Uh, I don't know," simply because you weren't confident about how many sons I have. You've met Asher. I, his father, introduced him to you. You should have said, "Yeah, Addison has a son."

In a similar way, we need to be confident in the things God has revealed to us. When God's *rhema*, his spoken or revealed word, comes alive in us, it would be foolish to deny its substance. We can and should have conviction—a firm belief—in the things God's Spirit reveals to us through his Word.* We can find conviction in our partial understanding. In fact, we cannot thrive without such conviction.

* The Holy Spirit (the One who gives *rhema*) will not reveal something that is contrary to Scripture. There are, however, times when our understanding of Scripture needs to be challenged and sharpened. An underdeveloped understanding of Scripture may cause us to think God's *rhema* is contradicting his *logos* (written Word). This is one of the many reasons spending time in God's Word is so important. The Spirit's leading will cause us to dive deeper into biblical truths so we can find a more complete understanding of truth. We need both *rhema* and *logos* if we are to discover the deep things of God.

But we lose credibility when we claim to know things about God (or truth) that he has yet to reveal to us.

Going back to the kid analogy, you would lose credibility if you asserted that I have *only* one son after meeting Asher. Such a statement would be false because I have two sons. You have turned a partial truth—that I have a son—into a falsehood by saying that I have only one son. In this instance, your knowledge, while true, became a detriment because it was improperly applied.

How often have we seen the church's "knowledge" of God wielded to bring pain and confusion? How many people have run from their Father's embrace because their siblings have stoned their path? The world rejects God when our arrogance gets the better of us. Our insecurity and fear of the unknown become our downfall. Don't forget that it's God's kindness that leads people to repentance (the return to their True Self). When we embrace humility and confidence, we both model for and invite others to move forward, finding their place in Christian community.

## TWO EXTREMES

I often find these two extremes among people today:

1. People who refuse to acknowledge or accept truth because they're terrified of what they don't know.
2. People who use what they do know to simplify and systematize everything they don't know.

In most cases, the truth is not found in either extreme. Profound revelation requires both a childlike wonder and a childlike faith. Our wonder acknowledges that there are things beyond our finite comprehension. Our faith acknowledges that what we do know or, I should say, who we know will guide us in our exploration of the infinitely wonderful.

Truth is not subjective, but its discovery is subject to a journey.

We can have confidence in God's immutability—his unchanging nature. But we must realize that his Spirit is transforming our lives, and with that transformation comes new eyes—a new perspective of the world. At times, it may seem as if truth—which emanates from God—changes, but it doesn't. Rather, it's our view of truth that is maturing, expanding, or refocusing.

Never in my life have I been more confident about who God is and who I am in him. But at the same time, never have I possessed this much humility and eagerness to learn more about him. You'll find that the wisest people are those who realize how little they know. I can only pray and hope that in the decades ahead I will find greater humility, confidence, and wisdom.

If you get this paradox, your life will never be the same. Let me offer another illustration to drive the point home.

If you were given the following image of a terrain, would you be able to accurately guess the nature of the surrounding area? You could make some educated guesses, but are you guaranteed accuracy? Go ahead, make your guess, and then turn to the appendix before reading further.

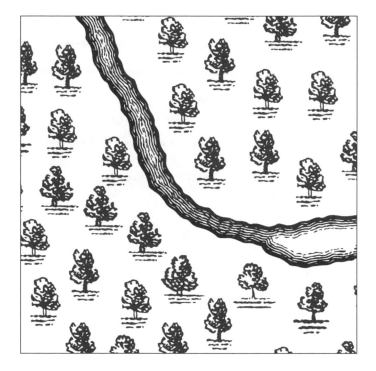

The illustration has many trees, so you likely assumed the presence of water and additional foliage. But, as you saw in the complete picture, the image is of an oasis in the middle of a desert that borders a mountain range.

Here's what happens. People make clever guesses about God and, for convenience' sake, put him and his ways into nice boxes. Now, there's nothing wrong with speculating about God. In fact, he desires that we make certain speculative efforts or guesses in our pursuit of him. But we get in trouble when we use what we do know to categorically define what we don't know. We have partial understandings of God's judgment, mercy, grace, love, holiness, and so on. But, as Eugene Peterson writes, "The fear-of-the-Lord prevents us from acting presumptuously and therefore destroying or violating some aspect of beauty or truth or goodness that we didn't recognize or understand."[4]

There are times when God's truths won't fit into our vernacular. Words won't always do God's ways justice. There are things I know about God that I don't know how to express. Maybe someday I'll learn how to, maybe I won't. I do know that God's wisdom is reshaping my life and changing my world. But this cannot happen if I do not take the dive into his otherness and get comfortable with humility. I must be like Isaiah and Ezekiel, completely undone by the presence of the Almighty, the One who knows the darkness of our hearts yet calls us worthy of his love.

## DIVE INTO FEAR

Psalm 33:8 says, "Let all the earth fear the LORD; let all the inhabitants of the world stand in awe of him!" This isn't a proclamation of dread—it's an invitation to intimacy. Every one of us has been invited to know God and be known by him.

There is an element of fear in every relationship, and we naturally fear what we do not understand. Each one of us is unique—an unknown sea of emotions, experiences, and genetics—so any relationship will provide its fair share of thrills and scares.

Even the beauty of God's love is terrifying when first encountered—his love is unlike anything we have ever known. But as we lose ourselves in his embrace, we find the peace and the security that transcend understanding and infuse our lives with faith and hope. This True Self life is found only in the fear-of-the-Lord, the most beautiful of intimacy.

The false safety of small living hasn't given you what you crave. You were made for more. Don't allow the lies of this world to create doubt in your heart. With God's Spirit, you can see your True Self and find the courage to abandon your whole being to him. Take the dive into fear, for it's in the intimacy of his holiness that we become his Saints.

> Behold, the eye of the LORD is on those who fear him,
>> on those who hope in his steadfast love,
> that he may deliver their soul from death. . . .
>
> Our soul waits for the LORD;
>> he is our help and our shield.
> For our heart is glad in him,
>> because we trust in his holy name.
> Let your steadfast love, O LORD, be upon us,
>> even as we hope in you. (vv. 18–22)

# THE S** WORD

*Sin is the rejection of love and life and truth.*
*—A. Stephan Hopkinson*

S in is a nasty subject. Even the way the word slithers off the tongue creates discomfort. We know it as the inflictor of shame. A reason for rejection. A destroyer of intimacy. A perversion of pleasure. Freedom gone terribly wrong. In so many ways, it strangles the very breath out of life. That's why most of us would prefer to just leave this nasty little word alone.

But there's much in Scripture about sin and its effect on our lives—specifically, how it distorts our humanity, attacking us on every meaningful front. In our pursuit of life, we'll have to tackle this difficult subject.

Growing up in church, I was always curious as to why certain sins were severely spoken against while others got swept under the rug. If you played your cards right, greed could get you on the church's board and in the front pew; after all, God's mission needs money.* But if you were navigating

---

* There is nothing wrong with making money. In fact, God puts gifts in people's lives to create wealth. Not everyone who has wealth is greedy. Greed has nothing to do with how much you possess. It has everything to do with how much your possessions possess you. Greed can be found in both the poorhouse and the penthouse.

same-sex attraction, you'd be discouraged from entering the building.

Something about this just didn't seem right.

It's painfully apparent that sin has been reduced to what happens when you "break the rules"—rules that seem both arbitrary (changing from context to context) and transient (here today, gone tomorrow). This has made us believe—and by "us" I mean both Christians and non-Christians—that we have the right to define what is and isn't sin. Not only that, but we've taken the liberty of creating a severity metric that allows us to either tolerate or ostracize people who struggle with certain sins.

There are many Hebrew and Greek words that are translated "sin" in the English Bible. Because we tend to use only our English word *sin* to capture the Hebrew and Greek, we inevitably flatten the ancient words, losing important nuance. For example, when the New Testament was written, the Greek word *hamartia* (translated "sin" in Scripture) could have been used to mean anything from an involuntary mistake to a serious offense against a god.[1]

This idea of sin is not as straightforward as we'd like to think, and that's probably another reason there is so much angst about it. Let's look at what the Greek and Hebrew words all have in common. In their commonality, we find the essence or central nature of sin.

In their original language, all the words translated "sin" in Scripture convey the idea of missing a target. Sometimes the target is clearly defined and understood; other times it isn't. But in either case, when the target is missed, there is a form of loss. Sometimes the loss isn't sensed because it is unknown or unrealized potential. Other times the loss is intimately known and the consequences immediately felt.

I've often heard sin defined as simply "missing the target (or mark)." This definition isn't wrong, but it is incomplete. When we consider sin as simply missing some target or law that often feels arbitrary, we can consciously or subconsciously discredit the value of hitting that target. But when we understand that sin causes us to both miss the target and suffer real loss, we look at it with new eyes and find courage to engage in fresh conversation.

We need to answer two questions: What is this target? And what do we lose or miss out on when we don't hit the mark?

## A PROMISE

> She will bear a Son, and you shall call His name Jesus [. . . which means Savior], for He will save His people from their sins [that is, prevent them from failing and missing the true end and scope of life, which is God]. (Matt. 1:21 AMPC)

Matthew's Gospel begins with seventeen verses of genealogy, followed by three verses of necessary setting, and ultimately climaxes with the great announcement that Jesus saves us from our sins, positioning us to find the life we were meant to know. (Keep in mind that this is the first New Testament verse to mention Jesus's identity and mission.)

I used to skip over the genealogy (yawn . . .). Who likes to read a bunch of names that are hard to pronounce? But then I realized the genealogy is important because it tells a story. Each one of the names represents a life, a promise, a seed. Each person is a chapter in a greater narrative.

It's easy for us to forget that the Old Testament is a story of love, dedication, and salvation. It's the story of the timeless covenant that creates buildup for the climactic cross—the fulfillment of God's covenant with us—the story of the generational struggle that has led to this moment in time.

Have you ever walked into a movie during the big reveal—that moment the entire movie has been moving its audience toward? If you missed the buildup, chances are the big moment didn't mean much. Without the movie's context—or history—it's easy to miss the moment and default to indifference or confusion. That's why history is so important. Karl Marx once wrote, "If you can cut the people off from their history, then they can be easily persuaded."[2]

If we've lost sight of where we've come from—our history as the people of God—is it possible that we've forgotten where we're going, the great covenant promise that God is moving us toward? Sin has always done its best to obstruct this promise.

✦ I ✦

Much happens between Genesis 1 and Genesis 11, but let's pick up the story in Genesis 12 with Abraham, with whom, interestingly enough, Matthew begins Jesus's genealogy.

God invites Abraham to set himself apart for a special purpose. With this purpose comes a covenant promise that

God will bless Abraham, his family, and ultimately the entire world through him. God promises that through Abraham's seed, a new family will be born, a family that supersedes geographic, ethnic, and generational barriers (Gen. 12; Rom. 4; Gal. 3).

It's evident when reading about Abraham's life that he sometimes loses sight of God's promises and design for his life. But God, despite Abraham's mishaps, continues to work with him, setting the stage for the ultimate story of redemption. This same narrative—in varying forms and degrees—continues in and through Abraham's descendants, eventually arriving at a little town with a manger. Despite Israel's infidelity and unbelief, God remains faithful to his covenantal promises, ultimately delivering the greatest twist of all time by becoming a member of Abraham's family to fulfill his covenant with Abraham and save us from sin's power.

Paul writes, "For our sake he made him to be sin who knew no sin, so that in him we might become the righteousness of God" (2 Cor. 5:21). The implications of these inspired words would take volumes to unpack. Because of its robustness, this verse is too often flattened, and the cross's narrative is limited to Jesus fulfilling a type of legal requirement—by never sinning and thus becoming a sacrifice for our sins—so we can go to heaven one day. While this is true, the cross also points back to the largeness of God's covenant promise to Abraham. The cross—which represents grace—is *also* an agent of promised empowerment: "For sin will have no dominion over you, since you are not under law but under grace" (Rom. 6:14).

Notice the juxtaposition of the ideas of law and grace. In a sense, the law points to our efforts to obtain freedom from sin—the things that steal life—in our own strength (Exod. 20). But grace points to God's covenant with Abraham. Grace is the evidence of God's promise to infuse us with his nature, giving us his power to rise above sin.

John tells us that "the law was given through Moses; grace and truth came through Jesus Christ" (John 1:17). This is a radical concept. Even back in the first century, there was confusion about the legal nature of the law (or Torah) and how it affected—or worked with—the covenant God made with Abraham. In his letter to the Galatians, Paul even had to point out that the covenant preceded the law by 430 years. Abraham, the father of faith, didn't have a list of rules that kept him from sinning. It was his faith—not his law keeping—that made him righteous, positioning him to receive God's covenantal purpose and promise.

Between Abraham and Jesus, the Torah (the law) came onto the scene. But that law is not the covenant. Nor is the covenant the law. This distinction is very important. The covenant is greater than the law. Jesus fulfilled both the law and the covenant through his life and death, but our understanding of salvation from sin gets confused if we lump these two together.

When we understand the covenant and its ultimate purpose as described in Scripture—to create a family that supersedes any boundary—we find an eternal *why* (or purpose) that positions us to live like Paul, becoming all things to all people while not violating the law of Christ (1 Cor. 9:19–22). The law of Christ was never meant to restrict freedom. It is for freedom that Christ has set us free. But his law does create the conditions of freedom.

The Torah offered a how for living—a how that evolved and matured with Jesus's life and death.

The covenant gives us a why for living—a why that was personified and made possible by Christ's life and death.

## CONTROL FREAKS

The religious leaders of Jesus's day had lost sight of the law's intent. In a real sense, they had forgotten that it pointed back to a greater covenant. Their forgetfulness was convenient because it helped justify their manipulation of the law to line their pockets and position themselves as God's elite. Jesus was quick to point out their abuse: "What sorrow also awaits you experts in religious law! For you crush people with unbearable religious demands, and you never lift a finger to ease the burden" (Luke 11:46 NLT).

These law experts were control freaks and used the law to subdue the people. They had made an idol of the law, not to mention they had added their own traditions and customs to adorn their favorite god. It's no wonder Jesus presented such a threat. His wisdom and actions undermined their elitism and exposed their idolatry. "Woe to you, scribes and Pharisees, hypocrites! For you tithe mint and dill and cumin, and have neglected the weightier matters of the law: justice and mercy and faithfulness. These you ought to have done, without neglecting the others" (Matt. 23:23). Simply put, there are weightier matters to God.

Despite popular belief, Jesus didn't disdain the law. In fact, never has a Jew been more true to the Torah. Remember, Jesus didn't come to abolish the law but to fulfill it.

Paul also makes it clear that the law is not inherently bad. He writes, "If a law had been given that could give life, then righteousness would indeed be by the law" (Gal. 3:21). The law isn't bad. It's just incapable of making us good.

The law falls short when it confines to words a way of living that can be known only by the Spirit. This is why Paul emphatically declares that "the letter kills, but the Spirit gives life" (2 Cor. 3:6). Again, words can be twisted, but the Spirit transcends contextual nuance.

I've seen Christians use God-breathed Scripture to condemn and demean. Even Satan quoted Scripture when tempting Jesus in the wilderness. This is why it's so important that we lean into the transforming power of the Spirit. He is the One who gives us the wisdom and the perspective to understand Scripture and navigate the billions of unique circumstances that seem to fall outside "the rules."

I once heard a professor argue that German Christians shouldn't have lied to the Nazis when asked if they were hiding Jews. He made the point that there are commands in Scripture that explicitly tell us not to lie. And you know what? He's right—that is, he's right about there being biblical instructions not to lie. Furthermore, Scripture does not offer explicit contingencies or provisions that allow us to lie in certain situations. But was the professor right about German Christians needing to tell the truth to the Nazis? No.

This story may seem absurd to you, but people actually think like this. It's an extreme example, but it shows what happens when people lose sight of God's greater purposes. These German Christians were committed to God's justice and were willing to lose their lives for it. Their actions were appropriate, selfless, and courageous. Telling the truth would have made them complicit in the devaluing and taking of human life, which is, as Jesus said, "a weightier matter."

I've watched Christians demean and belittle other Christians in the name of doctrine, hatred for sin, and "following the rules." Their nastiness is no different from that of the religious leaders who crucified Jesus. I guess we've forgotten that Jesus said the world would know him by our love for one another—not through our ability to find fault with one another. There is a place for disagreement and discussion, but it should be done within the context of relationship. Sadly, many of these disagreements now happen over social media—a hotbed of unchecked opinions that has depersonalized our interactions, causing us to devalue people by reducing them to a picture with a handle.

## WHERE RULES FAIL

> The law was our guardian until Christ came. . . . But now that faith has come, we are no longer under a guardian, for in Christ Jesus you are all sons [and daughters] of God, through faith. (Gal. 3:24–25)

Now that faith has come, we can lay hold of a new nature in Christ Jesus—the new heart that is capable of receiving the breadth of God's law (Ezek. 36; Jer. 31). The expression of our new nature's goodness cannot be confined to mere words. In fact, it will at times defy existing notions of propriety.

This is why Jesus was reticent about giving a bunch of rules. The truth is grace calls us to a higher standard—a standard that supersedes the confines of rules, a standard that goes beyond what we believe we're capable of. This is the big idea behind Matthew 5–7. Jesus was comparing life under the law and life under grace. The law created rules to govern behavior, but grace bypasses behavior to transform our hearts and motives.

Under the Torah, it was sinful to sleep with someone who was not your spouse. But under grace, we find the power to jettison lust and sexual perversion altogether.

Grace goes after the root of sin—our broken nature. The law just managed sin's fruit.

✦‡✦

Jesus constantly challenged the scribes' and Pharisees' notion of what was good and right. That's why these religious leaders would get so frustrated with him and accuse Jesus of impropriety, even though Jesus never broke God's law.

There was one Sabbath when Jesus met a man with a withered hand in a synagogue. The religious leaders were hopeful they would catch this charlatan doing work on the Sabbath. Jesus seemed to have a propensity for messing with their understanding of Sabbath law. The Pharisees had forgotten the Sabbath's purpose, which is to refresh and sustain life by reminding us that we're not gods of productivity. We didn't create this world, and it'll continue spinning without us.

To challenge their small-mindedness, Jesus called the deformed man to himself—embracing him in a clear, public demonstration—and discerning his accusers' intentions, he said, "Is it lawful on the Sabbath to do good or to do harm, to save life or to kill?" (Mark 3:4). But the experts in the law offered no response.

Jesus was angered and grieved by their hardness of heart. They clearly didn't care for their damaged brother and were more concerned about their precious understanding of the rules.

Without lifting a finger, Jesus healed the man. Technically, Jesus didn't do anything but speak, so he didn't violate the Sabbath. Yet the Pharisees "went out and immediately held counsel with the Herodians against [Jesus], how to destroy him" (v. 6).

Doesn't this seem absurd? We would never act in such a way, right?

Wrong. We're just as capable of this hypocrisy.

As human beings, we have a love-hate relationship with rules. We love rules because we love control. We hate rules because we love control. Basically, we're control freaks.

In theory, I don't mind the rules that govern our roads. After all, I don't want to get in a head-on collision because some guy is driving on the left side of the road. But when I get pulled over for going ten miles per hour over the speed limit, I can't help but view speed limits as arbitrary and as something that keeps our fine officers from attending to more important matters.

The Pharisees were the rule keepers, so they primarily loved the rules. That is, they loved *their* rules—the ones that maintained *their* status quo. They hated Jesus's new rules that required them to go beyond their comfort and shortsightedness.

Think about it. Why were the Pharisees threatened by Jesus? They were terrified of political repercussions. The Romans were already crucifying Jews at random and levying exorbitant taxes. This Jesus character presented the greatest threat yet because he talked of a new kingdom with new rules—an idea the kingdom of Rome would not take kindly to.

So the Pharisees used Jesus's apparent law breaking to shelter themselves from further Roman oppression. They had become self-absorbed control freaks, and Jesus threatened their law-oriented measures to keep the peace and save their skins. They were cowards, hiding behind a knockoff Torah.

When religious law becomes a means for self-preservation and comfort, there will be abuse and perversion. The purpose of God's law has always been to point us toward him. The rules were never intended to give us a license to point the finger at one another. We don't become more like God by figuring out how the people around us are unlike him. We become like God when we follow Jesus's example, taking up our crosses to embrace the royal law.

## ROYAL LAW

The royal law—also known as the law of liberty, Christ's law, the law of the Spirit, or the law of faith—is to be our new standard. It is the law of the covenant. To reject this new standard is to miss the mark and deny the breadth of

God's power to save and transform. The royal law brings God's holiness (or otherness) into focus. It invites us to become people of his otherness.

Jesus's invitation to deny ourselves, take up our crosses, and follow him is the new law (Matt. 16:24). This is the new way of being, marked by a primary love for God and others, on which "depend all the Law and the Prophets" (Matt. 22:40). But there's something different about this new law. It seems to be counterintuitive: to find life, you must die. At first glance, this new law seems strange. After all, isn't a law's purpose to protect the sanctity of life, not encourage death?

But as we know, Jesus's death redeemed death. He made death holy. Now death—specifically, death to self—is the law of new life.

Because of Jesus's life and death, we have been reborn with a new nature—his nature (2 Pet. 1:4). Now we can pursue a higher way of living—we can become Saints, people of his otherness. Otherness cannot *just* be taught; it must be caught. It must be discovered and known in Jesus's example and perfected through the work of his Spirit.

Remember, God's purpose is for us to follow in Jesus's footsteps, becoming priests and kings who reflect his justice, mercy, and faithfulness. When we take an attitude toward sin that says "*Since Jesus died for us, we don't have to give sin a second thought. We're forgiven and our sins are covered by the cross, so let's not talk about sin anymore,*" we miss the point.

The royal law doesn't excuse or belittle sin. In fact, the demands of holiness on our lives have not been lessened by the cross. They have been increased. But with this increase comes a greater measure of God's Spirit and grace. And now, through faith, we can be transformed into sons and daughters of God—reflections of his covenant promise to Abraham.

This is why Paul writes, "Do we then overthrow the law [Torah] by this faith? By no means! On the contrary, we uphold the law" (Rom. 3:31). Another way to put this is we uphold the law's original intent. Remember, Jesus said that he didn't come to abolish the law but to fulfill it. The law had three purposes: to serve as a guardian until Christ came, to distinguish Israel from other nations, and to create an awareness of humanity's incompleteness apart from God. The hope was that the law would lead us away from ourselves and into the arms of our Father.

God's Spirit, the One who knows all the nuances of the royal law, is constantly moving us toward life's ultimate target—union with God. The covenant, the law, Christ—all are about intimacy, purpose, and redemption. All are used by God to bring us to himself so that we can find our True Self, brimming over with the unique purpose and promise that he has placed within each of us.

When we turn to him, we become his priests—the people of his presence. We have received life, and out of our overflow, we can share that life with the world around us. But to turn away from God—to miss the mark—is to find hopelessness and despair. That's why God says that we "are destroyed for lack of knowledge; because you have rejected knowledge, I reject you from being a priest to me" (Hosea 4:6). The New Living Translation reads, "My people are being destroyed because they don't know me."

God was (and is) explicitly addressing an intimate knowledge of him. Israel had gone its own way, and their shortsightedness—a lack of divine vision—had caused them to live in ways that unmade them. So in an act of love, God rejected these false priests. The priests were supposed to spend their lives serving God, studying his ways, and representing him to the people. How could God allow them to continue in their priestly vocation when they refused to be intimate with his holiness?

The amazing news is that now, in Christ, we are priests, invited into God's presence. Because God's Spirit lives in us, we now have the capacity to know God intimately. God's grace—his covenant promise—opens our eyes to the beauty of holiness.

But the beauty of our new life will be hidden from us and the world we're called to reach if we flounder in and excuse sin. When we disregard God's command to live in holiness—which is to live according to the royal law or God's law as revealed in the person of Jesus—we are not rejecting an arbitrary target. We are missing the transforming power of God's grace and the work of his Spirit.

## FAMILY BUSINESS

God has always been about people. More specifically, he's always been about family—the original purpose of the covenant.

Jesus became the firstborn of many sons and daughters (Rom. 8:29), delivering us from the power of sin, giving us a spot at the royal table, and offering us a place in his heavenly mission—the mission to overwhelm the powers of this world with his love and holiness.

The covenant was never about keeping the rules. The covenant has always been an invitation to become the people of God, joining him in the rescue and restoration of the cosmos. We are re-created in God to become his ambassadors, reflecting God's restorative justice, love, and righteousness to our world.

The problem is that humanity (represented in Israel) couldn't quite grasp such an idea. We wanted to reduce life to the extent of our being—to the extent of self. We liked the idea of rules and regulations because it offered a form of self-mastery, and we love being our own masters. Because of our hard hearts, God made allowances. He knew that real life is found only in the loss of self, but he wouldn't impose his perfect will on us. His goal has always been to turn creatures into children, not robots. And such a transformation requires a measure of our participation.

Let's compare two verses that highlight the big difference between the law and the covenant:

You shall therefore lay up these words of mine in your heart and in your soul, and you shall bind them as a sign on your hand, and they shall be as frontlets between your eyes. (Deut. 11:18)

For this is the covenant that I will make with the house of Israel after those days, declares the Lord: I will put my law within them, and I will write it on their hearts. And I will be their God, and they shall be my people. (Jer. 31:33)

In Deuteronomy, we are the ones putting God's words in our hearts and souls. This is a "pick yourself up by your bootstraps" sort of thing. We're the ones doing the heavy lifting. This is our trying to keep the law in our own strength.

But in Jeremiah, God alludes to the Abrahamic covenant and mentions a future twist. He essentially promises to fulfill both parts of the bargain. He'll be the One who writes his law on our hearts, and he'll give us the power (grace) to live in covenant faithfulness.

Our reasonable response to this divine act of grace is to become people of faith (following in the footsteps of Father Abraham). In other words, the great act of faith is losing our lives to be found in God's. That's the beauty of grace. This is made possible by God's Spirit within—the promised Emmanuel, God with us: "I will give you a new heart, and a new spirit I will put within you" (Ezek. 36:26).

Now that Jesus has come and fulfilled God's covenant promise to Abraham (again, that's why Matthew begins Jesus's genealogy with Abraham), we can take up arms against the forces of evil. God's Spirit has made our hearts his home, and we are now members of his family—sons and daughters of the Most High—reborn of his nature (Rom. 8; 2 Pet. 1; 1 John 3), full of his life, and anointed to advance his kingdom purposes.

The cosmic rescue is underway.

# WORSHIP

We have a tendency to worship what we consider most noble, unique, or courageous about ourselves. Just look at Greek mythology or the heroes of our day. Self-worship is at the heart of sin. In fact, we're incapable of escaping the bonds of sin—bonds inflicted by our self-worship—without a measure of divine intervention.

That is why God put on flesh.

But it wouldn't do for God to become a man of our ideal form and type. Such a god would be too much like us, not enough unlike us. History boasts of many such extraordinary men—men who are fun to read and write about. These mighty men saved cities and even nations—but none of them was able to save the world.

Jesus was unlike the typical hero because he had to be.

Jesus didn't intimidate Rome, threatening fire if they didn't follow his lead. Rather, he became intimate with humanity's suffering and struggle, intimate to the point of death on a cross. In nakedness and shame, he gave his last breath.

Yet somehow Jesus's life epitomizes everything good we see in ourselves while still revealing a new type of good—a complex, simple goodness that confounds our best platitudes. As A. Stephan Hopkinson writes, "The fascination of the idea of God as revealed in and described by Jesus is that this idea is one I could never have wanted, because I could never have imagined it. . . . Any man interested in human life and concerned with human relationships can only say, 'Lord,' when he looks upon Jesus."[1]

Simply put, Jesus is too good to make up.

And the amazing part is he's offered both an example and the means for us to become Saints. In Jesus, we find a new humanity—the ultimate way of living that God is patiently and persistently moving us toward.

＋I＋

Throughout human history the fingerprints of God were upon them [humanity], yet they refused to honor him as God or even be thankful for his kindness. Instead, they entertained corrupt and foolish thoughts about what God was like. This left them with nothing but misguided hearts, steeped in moral darkness. Although claiming to be super-intelligent, they were in fact shallow fools. For only a fool would trade the unfading splendor of the immortal God to worship the fading image of other humans, idols to look like people, animals, birds, and even creeping reptiles! (Rom. 1:21–23 TPT)

The book of Romans is Paul's most complete discourse on the gospel (the good news of our salvation). It's only fitting Paul begins his letter by exposing what Jesus came to save us from. (Remember, Jesus's mission as described in Matthew was to save us from our *sins* and keep us from missing the true end and scope of life—which is God.) Following in Jesus's footsteps, Paul is committed to bypassing sin's expressions, which the law attempted to "manage," and striking straight at sin's heart.

And what do we find at sin's heart? Idolatry.

*Idolatry* is an antiquated term with seemingly little relevance to our Western way of life. That's probably why you won't hear many teachings on it. After all, when was the last time you saw someone worshiping a deer or bowing down to a statue?

But idolatry is just as pervasive today as it was when Paul penned his words to the Romans. Just look around . . . we want to be gods and goddesses in our own right—like God but apart from him, self-sufficient (we love that self!), worthy of worship, worthy of likes, mentions, and the praise of many. Besides, if idolatry was limited to a generational or cultural expression, I doubt we would find it in the first commandment: "I am the LORD your God, who brought you out of the land of Egypt, out of the house of slavery. You shall have no other gods before me" (Exod. 20:2–3). In fact, the remaining nine of the famous Ten Commandments are all related to symptoms of refusing to embrace this first commandment.

Idolatry is the lifeblood of sin.

Later in Exodus 20, God comments that he is a jealous God—specifically, jealous of our worship. I've known people who've taken issue with this idea of God being jealous. They picture God like one of the gods from Greek mythology—petty, narcissistic, and thriving on the worship of their subordinates. Only growing stronger in the love and adoration of their lessers.

But YHWH is nothing like Zeus, Poseidon, or Hades. He doesn't need our worship. Whether we worship him or not, YHWH remains God. If we refuse to worship him, the rocks will transform into something greater and find breath to sing his song.

Furthermore, God's position isn't threatened by our worshiping someone or something else. His jealousy is aroused by his love for us. He knows that by worshiping someone or something else, we are essentially unmaking ourselves. To worship something is to draw life from it, and there is no true life apart from God.

Humankind's undoing has always been our worship of self—our favorite idol. Our modern world is still very much in love with this idol. In fact, our Western culture celebrates and glorifies self-worship. This is why idolatry is deeply intertwined in the systems and pursuits of our world and undoubtedly alive and well today.

Is it any wonder that Jesus's call to life requires us to deny our self and follow in his *self*-sacrificing love? A new way of life made possible only by both his example and his Spirit?

Primitive worship of the sun or moon or nature was rooted in humankind's perception of those things. In other words, they worshiped their perception. They didn't actually worship the sun; they worshiped what they perceived as the sun. Nature is sublime, mysterious, and worthy of adoration, but its mystery and sublimity are signposts to its Maker (Paul's big point in Rom.

1:19–21). In a similar way, humankind is extraordinary, the apex of God's creation. But our brilliance is a reflection of God's nature and was never intended to be the object of our worship.

When we lose sight of this truth, we worship the creation rather than the Creator—the essence of idolatry and the birthplace of sin, separating us from the life, love, and promise found in the knowledge of God's true form and purpose.

## INSANE WORSHIP

The brilliance of our humanity grows in our worship of God, and sadly, the opposite is also true. "They were in fact shallow fools" (Rom. 1:22 TPT) could also be translated "they became insane."

This is literally what happened to King Nebuchadnezzar. In Daniel 4, we find an account of quite the human being. There was even a statue made to capture the image of this human god. But one day while basking in self-worship, this king lost his mind. And for the next seven years, Nebuchadnezzar behaved like an animal, becoming the laughingstock of his kingdom. This is the insanity effect Paul describes in Romans 1. When we worship ourselves, esteeming the extent of our being and knowledge above God's Word and ways, we begin to regress, returning to a primitive state of being. But when we approach God in faith (like Abraham), we expedite the process of becoming his mature children and the expression of his glory on the earth.

I love Nebuchadnezzar's story because it's ultimately an example of God's heart to redeem and restore. After seven years of behaving like an animal, Nebuchadnezzar "lifted [his] eyes to heaven, and [his] reason returned to [him], and [he] blessed the Most High, and praised and honored him who lives forever" (Dan. 4:34).

Let's look at the sequence of events, because Daniel was very careful with the details. The king first lifted his eyes to heaven. When Nebuchadnezzar lost his mind, he was surveying his kingdom from a rooftop. Essentially, he was looking down on what was seen and known. He was admiring the extent of his accomplishments.

But his deliverance came when he lifted his eyes to heaven—God's dimension, a place that was beyond the greatness of his achievements—and that's when his reason (or sanity) returned to him. When his sanity returned, he broke out in emphatic, prophetic declaration. And Scripture tells us that after his seven years of unmaking (the number seven, interestingly enough, conveys completion or wholeness), Nebuchadnezzar stepped into greater splendor and majesty.

You see, God's not trying to hog all the good stuff. He wants us to experience the best of life. There's nothing—including self—that God doesn't return better and brighter. He asks for our death so we can know life. He has greater glory in store for us than we could ever imagine, but we will not step into that glory if we hold on to our lives. In Christ, the only things we get to keep are the ones we freely give away.[2]

The refusal to worship self is the pathway toward what it means to be his Saints, the children who participate in the mystery of life. We are the evidence, here and now, of the future day when God's dimension invades what we now know as space, time, and matter. In that day, the rulers of this world—sex, stuff, and status—will be dethroned and placed within the beauty and purpose of their intended design. But we don't have to wait for that day; we can discover the beauty of God's design here and now.

God humbly took our form. If we are to be transformed into his image, we must clothe ourselves with humility. His humility requires ours.

There is no greater worship than dying to self. It's the only thing that will free us from the sin (idolatry) and sins (everything that stems from idolatry) that mar our world.

> I appeal to you therefore, brothers [and sisters], by the mercies of God, to present your bodies as a living sacrifice, holy and acceptable to God, which is your spiritual worship. Do not be conformed to this world, but be transformed by the renewal of your mind, that by testing you may discern what is the will of God, what is good and acceptable and perfect. (Rom. 12:1–2)

## REDEEMED FOR A PURPOSE

If we take a self-centric approach to sin and salvation, we will miss the bigger picture of grace and justification and, in a sense, succumb to the self-worship at sin's core. To understand the gravity of sin, we have to move beyond the boundaries of personal piety and right standing with God.

We must do the hard work to see ourselves within God's great story of redemption—our family business.

Our purpose is a holy purpose, and this purpose requires us to embrace the empowerment of grace, breaking the chains of sin. Chains that have kept us from realizing our true identity and experiencing the life God has for us. We find confidence in knowing that "the [Old Self] has no claims on us at all, and we have no further obligation to live in obedience to it. For when you live controlled by the flesh, you are about to die. But if the life of the Spirit puts to death the corrupt ways of the flesh, we then taste his abundant life" (Rom. 8:12–13 TPT).

God's Spirit has set us free from the power of sin. We can now become the mature children of God, moved by the impulses of his Spirit (v. 14). Since the beginning, we have been destined to become his sons and daughters (Eph. 1:4), not just in theory but in form and practice. And the world is longing to see this display of glorious life.

It's great that we sing about being children of God, but let's move beyond mere words and become his living poetry—people who reveal his kindness, grace, love, and holiness in both word and deed. The grace we've been given allows us to unveil a new way to be human.

## CHRISTLIKE CARICATURES

In 2015, I attended an online marketing conference. It was a massive gathering of introverts who specialized in monetizing virtual interactions. In other words, these people don't like being seen by people but enjoy making money off them. Even the speakers—you know, the ones in front of hundreds of people—possessed a surprising amount of self-deprecation and awkwardness. In fact, one speaker didn't make eye contact with the audience during his entire forty-five-minute session.

The conference hosts had the brilliant idea to bring in an artist who did caricatures. They must have thought the artist could heat up their melting pot of bubbling personalities.

Well, I'm a sucker for caricatures. It's one of the few depictions of me that I can look at and know, beyond a shadow of a doubt, that I don't look *that* bad. So I got in line. And so did two of the other people with me (the third wisely abstained from such imprudent behavior).

My brother Austin was one of the two people in line with me. Now, Austin is a really good-looking guy—and this is not brotherly bias. When it was Austin's turn to have his face distorted by the pen, the cynical mastermind began giggling like a fourth grader who just read a juicy love note passed behind her teacher's back. After about three minutes of calculated heinousness, the artist, with a wry grin, handed Austin his work of art.

Let's just say the caricature looked like it could have been the offspring of the Geico caveman. Everything was wrong about Austin's face: his teeth were too big, his hair too curly, his nose all wrong, his bone structure ape-like. Though Austin is attractive, I seriously doubt any woman would be attracted to Austin's caricature. It was that bad.

But there was something about the caricature that resembled Austin. I could even tell the caricature was of Austin and not of some random conference Joe. While the caricature was grotesque, it did—in a strange way—reflect its inspiration.

When we call ourselves "Christians" (little Christs), we claim a new identity. We claim a new inspiration, a new source of life. But when we shrink back from who God has re-created us to be, we become Christlike caricatures. We may bear a faint resemblance, but that semblance becomes a point of mockery: "The name of God is blasphemed . . . because of you" (Rom. 2:24).

We insult the finished work of the cross when we refuse to embrace its transforming power. In fact, Paul writes that we become enemies of the cross when we deny its ability to renew us (Phil. 3). And that's why the greatest social injustice facing our world today is not human trafficking or poverty or corrupt politicians or global debt. The greatest social injustice facing our world today is our refusal to become the expression of Christ on the earth. Period.

## NEW CREATION

The cross represents our new life. More specifically, it represents our new life in Christ. In this new life, we find the power to transcend the cares and concerns of this world. We find the grace to become the people of God, bearing the true mark of any believer—holiness. Paul boldly writes, "Far be it from me to boast except in the cross of our Lord

Jesus Christ, by which the world has been crucified to me, and I to the world. For neither circumcision counts for anything, nor uncircumcision, but a new creation" (Gal. 6:14–15).

It's all about new creation. This idea of new creation animates Paul's letters. It is the wind in his sails—the great mystery made possible by Christ's death and resurrection. May we never get over the fact that we are now sons and daughters, partakers of God's divine nature.

I hope you now see that a life of sin steals our humanity. A life of self-worship is a caricature, not a true reflection. But grace saves us from the power of sin. Because Jesus laid down his life, we can lay down our sins.

God's will is for us to walk in purity, which is complete freedom from anything that abases: "For God has not called us for impurity, but in holiness. Therefore whoever disregards this, disregards not man but God, who gives his Holy Spirit to you" (1 Thess. 4:7–8).

Sadly, because we have such a low view of God's saving power, we haven't embraced the call to holiness. We view holiness as a destination. We make it a status that is obtained only by following the rules. But as you now know, holiness is so much more than that. The journey of holiness is a dive into the fullness of God's new creation life. It is to lose ourselves in the new humanity found in Christ.

As I said earlier in this book, I think we're terrified of discovering that we are, in fact, made for wonder. Our divine brilliance is shrouded by unbelief, truncated theology, and a lack of imagination. Even in our "salvation," it seems we cannot see beyond the confines of our fallen nature.

It's time we take back what is ours. Jesus came to give us life in its fullness. The question is, Will we receive with humility the grace that restores our vitality? In other words, Will we get over ourselves and become fully alive—fully human? Or will we run from the beauty and otherness of our promised new nature—our True Self in Christ?

The world will believe in the divine when they see Christ in us.

## BACK TO FAMILY

The whole point of new creation is for us to become children of God, partakers of his otherness (holiness), reflecting his life to overwhelm the darkness in our world. The goal isn't just for us to "make it to heaven one day." When we make "getting to heaven" our only aim, we deny ourselves the power, calling, and promise that God has made available in this lifetime. I believe this is why so many Christians struggle with discouragement and a lack of vision for their lives.

We were created for an eternal purpose, a purpose that reaches into our temporal lives and infuses them with meaning. "Beloved, we are God's children right now; . . . all who focus their *hope* on [Jesus] will always be purifying themselves, just as Jesus is pure" (1 John 3:2–3 TPT, emphasis added). One reason many Christians aren't walking in freedom from sin is because they have no hope (or they have a lack of hope).

People perish from a lack of vision or hope (Prov. 29:18). I'm sure you've heard this idea before, maybe in a vision meeting or corporate setting. What's interesting is we find this verse sandwiched between two verses on correction. Solomon is challenging us to have a vision for something greater than us. You'll never welcome correction if you can't see beyond your current being.

We need God's Word and the people in our lives to remind us that there is something greater than we have known, seen, or given ourselves to.

Our hope, that vision, is ultimately found in Jesus. That's why in Hebrews 12, immediately following a commentary on Jesus's glorious death, we find the idea of God disciplining us because he loves us as sons and daughters. The writer even says that we are illegitimate children if our lives lack the tension that comes with discipline.

God's saving purposes extend beyond conversion and into our very real, everyday lives. God doesn't save us just from a metaphysical hell; he saves us from the hell that our sins create in the present. Don't try to tell me that sin doesn't have consequences now that you are "in Christ." Spend a week stealing, cheating, gossiping, lying, abusing, and so on and see what kind of prison that creates. God's grace saves us from the eternal, penal ramifications of sin, *and* it empowers us to step into life now.

⁘

God uses a vision of who he's created us to be to create tension in our lives, a tension that comes from knowing there's more to life. We're told to "lay aside every weight, and sin which clings so closely, . . . looking to Jesus the founder and perfecter of our faith" (Heb. 12:1–2). In Jesus, we have both the example and the empowerment.

When we fail to die to self and embrace our true nature as sons and daughters, we experience the Lord's discipline. This discipline leads us to him. It is "for our good, that we may share his holiness" (v. 10). God disciplines us because his love won't allow him to be casual about the sins that steal our vitality.

So many Christians see Jesus *only* as their Savior, the One who put them in right standing with God. And this is undoubtedly true. But it doesn't stop there; that's merely the beginning.

In Jesus, God revealed that we are destined "to be conformed to the image of his Son, in order that [Jesus] might be the firstborn among many" (Rom. 8:29). Jesus lived a fully human life, free from the bondage of sin. And that is God's intent for us. Until we realize that ultimate aim, we will learn obedience in pain (Heb. 5:8).

Please understand that I am not suggesting voluntary austerity or pain. Rather, I'm making the point that God cares more about what's happening *in* us than what's happening *to* us. Don't get me wrong; he cares about both. But like any good parent, he doesn't compromise our future by pacifying our present.

God cares about what happens to us *now*. He wants us to experience life in its fullness *now*. He's given us grace to rise above sin *now*. There are people who need to see God's holiness revealed through us *now*.

That's why this battle against sin is so important.

We overcome sin through humility: "As you yield freely and fully to the dynamic life and power of the Holy Spirit, you will abandon the cravings of your self-life" (Gal. 5:16 TPT). Before Christ, the aim was to manage sin by not breaking the Torah. But now that we are reborn with God's Spirit—the Spirit of Christ—we can soar above the power of sin.

## CHILDREN OF GOD

John, the disciple whom Jesus loved, tells us that anyone who continues to sin doesn't know God intimately as his child (1 John 3:4–7). These people who go on sinning haven't taken the dive into fear.

They have made an idol of God—a god who supports their small thinking. They are "worshiping" a safe god who doesn't have the power to save them completely. They make God in their own image and then wonder why he's not transforming them.

They have yet to know true freedom. Could it be they are not walking in freedom from sin because they have a low view of God and his plan to rescue humanity?

The beloved disciple then escalates his point by saying that anyone who is given over to sin is of the devil, because Satan was the first one to worship someone or something other than God (v. 8). John is not saying that anyone who sins is of the devil. Rather, John is describing a condition in which someone is serving sin, making sin their master.

But "everyone who is truly God's child will refuse to keep sinning because God's seed [Greek *sperma*] remains within him, and he is unable to continue sinning because he has been fathered by God himself" (v. 9 TPT). That is God's promise for us. We will be his children, possessing his nature (his DNA) and walking in freedom from sin. We must make that our target. Any other idea of *life* will lead to frustration and dissonance.

You might be thinking, *Addison, that's an impossible standard—a standard that will frustrate the best of God's Saints.* But if our salvation through Jesus Christ is true, then John's message is true. If we count on the first, we can trust the second.

Verse 9, so often used to condemn people, was actually meant to inspire us. It's a reminder that we have a new nature, infused with God's life and grace. A new nature that doesn't have to succumb to sin's smallness. God's seed is in us. We are his offspring, full of new life.

An apple seed doesn't look anything like an apple. Nor does it resemble a tree. But give the seed time and the right conditions, and you will see your apple.

God's holiness is imprinted on our new nature. If given time and the right conditions of faith, hope, and love, our True Self will emerge from its shell of fallen humanity, revealing our Father's redemptive power to a world that's waiting on tiptoe to see it.

John continues: "The beautiful message you've heard right from the start is that we should walk in self-sacrificing love toward one another. . . . Jesus sacrificed his life for us. Because of this great love, we should be willing to lay down our lives for one another" (vv. 11, 16 TPT).

Inspired by God's Spirit, John brilliantly weaves together themes of sin, self-sacrifice, family, and love. Because we have the security of being God's children, we can embrace the process of becoming mature sons and daughters, dying to self-worship and its consequent sins, ultimately finding our True Self in the arms of Life.

The whole point is family. God so loved the world that he gave his only Son to make many sons and daughters. God gave his Son to fulfill his promise to Abraham, which was to bless the cosmos through his offspring, Jesus, the Savior of the world. And now that Jesus has done what only he could do, we are redeemed and empowered to join the family business, reclaiming our world from the powers of sin and death.

This is why the New Testament calls us to a higher way of living.

## SIN'S SMALLNESS

Paul writes that "our old self was crucified with [Christ] in order that the body of sin might be brought to nothing, so that we would no longer be enslaved to sin" (Rom. 6:6).

So many people view the Christian life as mere abstinence from sin. But that perspective has very little power. The transcendent holiness that is ours in Christ "is not (as people often imagine) a matter of denying something good. It is about growing up and grasping something even better."[3]

Life shouldn't be about what we run from. It should be about what we run toward. The best "no" is a strong "yes."

Since we are now the righteousness of God in Christ Jesus (another way of saying we are part of his family, receiving the fullness of his faithfulness to the covenant), we can step into the fullness of being, which includes freedom from sin. We can say "Yes!" to our New Self in Christ and by doing so say "No!" to the power of sin.

The problem is that whether we're afraid to talk about sin or we can't stop talking about it, we've made sin the focus. When we don't talk about sin—a major theme in Scripture—it becomes the scary monster that lives in our grandma's attic. We all know it's nesting above our heads, but no one wants to confront it.

Our focus should be that God has invited us into his family, and because he loves us, he desires to free us from both the punishment and the power of sin: "For the wages of sin is death, but the free gift of God is eternal life in Christ Jesus our Lord" (v. 23).

When we see sin within this familial context, we're not afraid to talk about it or address its symptoms because we see it for what it is. Sin distorts genuine humanness, which means it distorts the image of God. It needs to be addressed. It needs to be confronted. But we must do so from a place of love and compassion. If we are to reveal God to our world, then we must work to see ourselves—and one another—the way God sees us.

When we capture God's heart, we will, by the power of his grace, cast off the sins that make our lives small. As we do this, we'll find the love and conviction to invite others into wholeness and holiness (which is kind of the whole point of the Great Commission).

✦I✦

When we refuse to worship our Old Self—turning from the natural image it so relentlessly puts before us—our eyes open to the True Self. This turning from the Old Self for the awakening of the New Self is the pathway of holiness—the journey of discovering God's otherness. It reorients our worship, positioning us to receive from the only one who is worthy. As we lean into God's otherness, our lives are transformed, sin loses its power over us, and the world—which God loves—gets to see his justice, love, and mercy animated in our lives.

Our sins didn't just create a metaphysical debt that had to be paid. Sin is a flaw in the human condition. A flaw that comes with the freedom of choice. A flaw that is fixed only by the life of our new humanity—the life found in the blood of our older brother, the only person who got this whole humanity thing right.

The man who died for our sins now offers death to sin.

I don't know about you, but give me the liberty that comes with such a death.

# GOD'S LOVE LANGUAGE

I t was a beautiful summer evening. Sunlight was cascading across the sky, turning clouds vibrant shades of orange and red. I was sitting on a curb enjoying the light show while watching Asher, my firstborn, attempt to ride a tricycle. His feet couldn't reach the pedals, yet he wouldn't stop trying. A great sense of joy and pride was welling up in me as I witnessed his resilience. It was a good night.

As I was experiencing this pride in my son, God suddenly dropped something into my spirit. I heard the words *I am love*. Now, I've been in church my whole life, and I've heard this idea of God being love a few times. So when God whispered those words into my spirit, it's not like I was hearing anything I hadn't heard before. But I threw aside my preconceived ideas and asked God to reveal something new to my heart. I specifically asked God to reveal a facet of his love I had yet to experience or comprehend.

As I quieted myself, I sensed God was showing me something about his love language.

*I am love, and faith is my love language.*

How fascinating.

But then my left brain—the logical side—kicked in, and I thought, *Faith isn't one of Gary Chapman's five love languages, so it obviously can't be God's love language.*

If you aren't familiar with the five love languages, then none of this is making any sense. So let me quickly explain what they are. If you are familiar with them, just skip the next paragraph.

The five love languages represent the ways we like to give and receive love. They include quality time, acts of service, physical touch, gifts, and words of affirmation.[1] The idea is once you figure out someone's preferred love languages, you can show them love in ways they appreciate. I'm a big acts of service guy, but acts of service don't do anything for my wife. I'll spend hours cleaning the house, and she'll hardly notice my efforts.

Okay, back to my story.

For a while, I just sat there, trying to sort it all out. God's love language. Hmm, I missed that one in systematic theology. This whole thing seemed a bit weird. But then I remembered a verse from the book of Hebrews: "Without *faith* it is impossible to please him, for whoever would draw near to God must believe that he exists and that he rewards those who seek him" (11:6, emphasis added).

*That's it*, I thought. *God, we please you by our faith. And since we please you by our faith, that's how we show that we love you. Just like how spending quality time with my wife shows her I love her.*

I expected to hear the spiritual equivalent of "Nailed it!" but I could tell I was still missing what God was trying to show me.

I just quieted myself and waited. And waited. And waited. Nothing came to me. So I took Asher inside to get him ready for bed.

Later that night, the whole point of the love language revelation hit me in the face. Not literally, of course, but it did rock me. (Again, not literally.)

God showed me that faith isn't just how we show our love for him—although God does find great pleasure in our faith because of what it does *in* us. Rather, the whole idea of faith being God's love language is about how he shows his love *to* us.

As usual, my initial response was to make the revelation about me—my effort, my spiritual muscle. But God was trying to show me that it wasn't about me proving my love for him through my faith. It was about me receiving his love by acknowledging his faith in me.

This took me back several verses to Hebrews 11:1: "Now faith is the assurance of things hoped for, the conviction of things not seen."

Faith isn't just an obscure spiritual concept. It's concrete, born of conviction. A conviction that escapes the prison of the present. A conviction that's energized by a truth that will reshape the present, bringing forth a new reality.

## FAITH, HOPE, AND LOVE

So now faith, hope, and love abide. (1 Cor. 13:13)

Hope is the vision. Faith is the power. Love is the why.

Jesus lived and died to show us the true form of faith, hope, and love. That is why we are to look "to Jesus, the founder and perfecter of our faith, who for the joy that was set before him endured the cross" (Heb. 12:2).

Jesus had (and has) a vision for us. A vision of us seated with him. A vision of us becoming reflections of his glory. A vision of us developing the capacity to see and know his love, so we can share that love with those who have no vision.

Jesus is the perfecter of our faith. He is also the evidence of God's faith in us.

Think about it. God sent Jesus before you ever took a step toward him. Before you ever did anything good, God's sword—the cross that reclaimed our world for Christ—was driven deep into the ground, revealing God's faith in our humanity.[2]

The cross doesn't just represent redemption. It also tells the story of God's faith, steadfast love (a frequent theme in the Psalms), and patient endurance. He will not give up on us. Even when we are faithless—he is faithful. The word *faithful* originally conveyed the idea of being full of faith (like how *hopeful* means full of hope). We now use it to mean loyal, and it certainly does mean that too. But faith is the bedrock of loyalty.

God is faithful, so he is committed to the object of his faith. You cannot have faith without an object—a person or outcome—that your faith is attached to. Without the object, faith is meaningless because it has no substance.

God has faith in you because he sees you in Christ. He's confident in the work of his Spirit. He's confident he can finish the good work he started. His faithfulness is not contingent on your worthiness. Simply put, God's full of faith because he knows what *he's* capable of—he doesn't struggle with false humility or doubt.

The question is, Will you accept his faith in you? Will you embrace the hope he's placed on and in you? Or will you run from who he has created you to be and reject the experience of his transforming love?

Let me be clear: nothing can separate you from God's love (Paul is emphatic about that point in Rom. 8). But pride and idolatry will block the experience of his love. God does not impose his will on us—even when that will is for us to know his love and share that love with others.

## GOD AND LOVE

As we've seen throughout this book, God is the most dedicated Father. His dedication reaches through time to touch every generation, culture, and continent. Human history is a story of family told through families, each family adding depth and breadth to God's love story. "For God so *loved* the world [*kosmos*], that he gave his only Son" (John 3:16, emphasis added). In other words, Love became a man so we might know love.

I often hear people say that God is love, quoting 1 John 4:8. And nothing could be more true. God is love. Perfect love is the blood in his veins. It's the why behind his every what. It is the greatest of the everlasting three—faith, hope, and love—because it is the most central to his nature.

But have we made an idol of love? Have we reduced God to our idea of love rather than allowing his Spirit and Word to transform our understanding of love?

*Love* is our greatest idol. And if you think about it, that makes sense. If love truly is the highest and best, then when it falls, it would naturally fall the lowest.

The enemy of our souls specializes in perversion. And there's no question that his perversion of love is his highest and best. Just look around. There's no virtue with more distortions.

God is love. But love is not God.

✦—I—✦

Love is patient. (1 Cor. 13:4)

When I think of God, I can't help but be astounded by his patience. We make a mess of things. (Often, we make a mess of things in his name.) Yet he doesn't reject us. He works with us. His Spirit ever offers new eyes to see and a new vision.

But we often flee from his vision. It's too grand. Too beautiful. Too demanding. We run back to ease and comfort, hoping to find the good life somewhere else. But it's nowhere else to be found. Again, God's Spirit calls us back, gently, faithfully: *Open yourself to my love. My grace is sufficient for you.*[3]

But this invitation seems like nonsense. It's impractical. It's unrealistic. God, there's no way you created us for *that*. We are mere mortals. Who are we that you are mindful of us? We don't want your eyes on us—we prefer the shadows, even if they hide the light within.

Yet God is patient, faithful to his vision for our lives. But not because he's a controlling Father who wants things done his way. He's not going to demand our participation because he lives vicariously through us and finds worth in our success. No, it's not that at all. He is in the fabric of our being. He can't help but feel our tension.

So what does he do? He adds his faith, hope, and love to our tension—awakening a sense of new life in us. He is awakening us to our True Self and giving us a new hope. Or I should say, bringing us back to the old hope that was written on our hearts.

We run from that hope because it creates more tension in our lives. But we cannot have hope without tension. With hope comes the awareness that things will change. They must change—for something greater is on the horizon. Something greater is within. We can see it, feel it.

We can lean into the tension, or we can run from it. Like pulling a resistance band, the more we run, the greater the tension.

His patient love invites us closer. Closer to the consuming fire, the fire that hurts less when we get lost in its flames. When we run from his fire, his love doesn't relent. It arrests our world, opening our eyes to the futility and meaninglessness of existence without Life. We think we want self-sufficiency, freedom from the big bad man in the sky. But we couldn't be more wrong. In our running, we find ourselves chasing shadows of his goodness, believing the moon offers a light of its own.

Through it all, our good Father patiently watches over us, his providence never imposing on our free will. After all, he created us to become sons and daughters, not robots. That vision keeps him from interfering with us. That vision fills him with patience.

One of the things that makes God *God* is that he knows the end from the beginning. His foreknowledge is a central part of his otherness. And he invites us to see our world through his eyes. His Word tells us the final story, and he invites us to build for that great finale. We build for it with faith, hope, and love. We build for it by the power of his Spirit and the beauty of his grace.

We do all this with patience, knowing that he who began a good work in us will bring it to completion, that the day will come when God's righteousness, justice, love, and mercy will rule the nations. There will be a day when every tear will arrive at its intended design. Every heart will know as it is now known. Creation will be rescued from decay—and the manifest presence of our God will open every eye. "Love is patient . . . ; love never ends" (1 Cor. 13:4, 8).

We are invited to see one another through this vision. And to see ourselves through this hope, discovering what it means to be Saints. This shift of perspective will inevitably create tension in our lives and in our relationships. After all, we are not as we should be. This world has gone astray.

How do we—as the people of God—build for the vision God has spoken over us? We do it carefully, intentionally, prayerfully, patiently.

Watching closely, you begin to learn the rhythms of grace. You see God in action in your life, and you ask him to give you the subtlety, the brilliance, the nuance to share his good news. The news that this world isn't right, our souls aren't right, and God, in his mercy, is calling us to repentance, to a new way of being human. He is also calling us to join the family business of salvation, forgiveness, and restoration.

This is Love. This is our God. There is no one like him.

## LOVE FOR FREEDOM

We've seen how frail and fickle human love can be. We find it hard to believe a love rooted in selfless devotion—and not some cultural, generational, or political agenda—is possible. Too often "love" is used to manipulate and control, to conform the object of its affections to "ideal" behaviors. But this is a selfish love.

Love's true aim is freedom—freedom from anything that abases.

That's it. True love has no other motive.

When most people think of purity, they think of sexual purity. But purity is so much more than abstaining from illicit sexual behaviors. Purity is complete freedom from anything that steals your vitality. This kind of purity requires a process—a refiner's fire, if you will. And every process requires patience.

Again, we find ourselves confronted with this idea of patience. It's inseparable from true love. And like love, its goal is freedom.

You see, patience doesn't compromise. It holds its ground. That's why steadfastness is its twin sister. In these two, you'll find so much confidence—so much hope. And because patience is fueled by faith and hope, it extends a helping hand. It offers kindness and understanding. Patience is not afraid of the messy.

✦⟊✦

In the eighth chapter of John, we find Jesus relaxed, seated, and surrounded by a large crowd. He's doing his usual thing—teaching about the kingdom—when suddenly a group of religious leaders crashes the party. They've found the perfect opportunity to put him on the spot. Somehow, these guys have caught a woman in the very act of adultery, and they want Jesus's opinion on what should be done with her.

The Pharisees want to stone her, and they are using their understanding of the law to justify their position. In Jesus, they see someone who is weak. A man full of lofty ideas but lacking any backbone. *This is our moment of triumph*, they think. *The people will finally see this Jesus for who he really is—a fake.*

Their temperatures are rising. Their hearts are racing. People are looking for stones.

But, as usual, Jesus does something surprising. He doesn't say a word. He doesn't even get up. He just starts scribbling in the sand—unrushed, unhurried, patient.

Of course, this infuriates the Pharisees. They demand answers. They want Jesus to pick a side. Finally, he speaks. Unfazed, Jesus stands and says, "Let him who is without sin among you be the first to throw a stone at her" (v. 7).

Then, with nothing more to say, he returns to the ground and continues writing in the sand.

There are many theories about what Jesus wrote in the sand. No one can know for sure, but the most compelling explanation I've heard suggests that he wrote a verse from Jeremiah 17 to expose the religious leaders' hypocrisy:

> O LORD, the hope of Israel,
>     all who forsake you shall be put to shame;
> those who turn away from you shall be written in
>         the earth,
>     for they have forsaken the LORD, the fountain
>         of living water. (v. 13)

It's interesting that in John 7, just a chapter earlier, Jesus was teaching on this living water. Is there something to the proximity of these two accounts? I think so.

Jesus's words—both written and oral—clearly have an effect on those present. The accusers begin to leave, with the wisest and oldest leaving first. These men are probably most aware of their hypocrisy. Most aware of their internal struggle—the dissonance that plagues their souls.

After everyone leaves, Jesus stands up and looks at the woman. This is a really interesting detail. While her accusers were present, Jesus mostly remained in the dirt. But once these false judges leave the scene, the only One who has any right to judge her stands to his feet. It's time for Jesus to assume his rightful role as judge over her life. He's prepared to offer his verdict. His words have power.

From this place of authority, he looks at her and says, "'Woman, where are they? Has no one condemned you?' She said, 'No one, Lord.' And Jesus said, 'Neither do I condemn you; go, and from now on sin no more'" (8:10–11).

What a beautiful demonstration of faith, hope, and love. What a surprising portrayal of patience. Jesus's words both sting and heal her. His words cut deeper than the Pharisees' accusations, traveling to the depths of her soul. She knows she's guilty, but Jesus offers new life. And with this new life, he requires everything from her. His love revealed through faith now makes the impossible possible. And with this faith comes the miraculous power for her to go and sin no more.

Notice that Jesus implicitly accuses the woman of sinning. He's not afraid to call sin *sin*. He doesn't say, "Don't worry about your sin because my grace will cover it all." Jesus, more than anyone, knows that sin has a cost. And he won't feed the darkness in this woman's heart. He is light. And light reveals truth.

Jesus has a vision for this woman—he has hope for her. And that's why he won't condemn her. He calls out the sin—and condemns it—but he refuses to condemn her.

The Greek word translated "condemn" in this passage means, in the most basic sense, to sunder, to part, to sift, ultimately to divide out.[4] In other words, it means to reject—with a profound sense of finality. The Pharisees initially propose such a judgment. But Jesus, as the woman's true judge, refuses to label her as a failure. Yes, she had failed. But her journey was far from over. Rather than condemning her, he invites her to condemn or part from the sin that had caused her shame.

True freedom was hers.

All this was made possible because Jesus had a patient hope. Jesus was willing to see beyond her present and fight for her future. And this is what he does for each of us. This is his love language—love revealed in patient hope and faith. He sees us not as we are but as we could be. Paul had just such a personal revelation of the mystery of God's patience. That's why he writes, "But I received mercy for this reason, that in me, as the foremost, Jesus Christ might display his *perfect patience*" (1 Tim. 1:16, emphasis added).

Jean Vanier wrote that true love is "to reveal the beauty of another person to themselves."[5] Jesus knows that if you treat a person as they are, they will remain as they are. But if you treat them as they could and should be, they will become something more. That is why Scripture constantly reminds us of who we are in Christ. It is an invitation to that something more.

## TOLERANCE AND PATIENCE

The question is, Do we believe in that something more? Are we willing to patiently fight for it? Will we hope against hope? Will we trust God's faith in us?

Our world demands tolerance because it has no hope. It doesn't know to believe for a better tomorrow. It's just trying to manage and appease the pains of today. The wholeness that God has for us, the perfection toward which his love guides us, requires a process. This process brings us to the end of our False Self and opens our eyes to the wonders of life, love, and truth.

But we'll reject this process (it's painful!) when we lose sight of its purpose—complete freedom from anything that steals life. That is love's aim—the wholeness of its beloved.

There are so many people in our world who need us to show them real love. They need us to love them enough to not merely offer vacuous answers, devoid of real conviction. These people—our family members, friends, coworkers, and so on—need us to get our hands dirty. To get outside our Christian boxes. To break the rules while never violating the law of Christ. This kind of patient love does not look down on others with contempt. It gets down in the sand to garner perspective and understanding. It requires us to find those who are not easy to love. But it refuses to compromise. It refuses to call good evil and evil good. This love wants more than false peace—it's not after political correctness. It's in pursuit of deep transformation.

Tolerance may get in the sand—if it's the popular or easy thing to do—but it never gets back up. It never calls us to something greater because it lacks faith and hope.

A tolerant Jesus would have saved the woman from the religious bigots only to send her on her way, none the wiser that she was capable of so much more. It wouldn't have been long before she found herself back in her old ways.

But Jesus's message of patient forgiveness told her that the sin could be left behind. It brought her back to her True

Self. A desire to find life, meaning, and connection had driven her into the arms of adultery. Jesus showed her that she indeed was made for these things, but she was going about it all wrong. He gave her a glimpse of what real love looks like—then he invited her to change her ways, to go and sin no more.

> Precisely because forgiveness is forgiveness and not mere tolerance, it must go with an implacable refusal to collude with sin, with violence or prejudice or spite, with pride or greed or lust, with any of the things that deface and corrupt God's good and beautiful creation.[6]

You see, patience doesn't condemn, but it sure does convict. It convicts because it creates tension in our lives. Tension that can lead us to the death of our False Self. Jesus didn't condone or tolerate the woman's decision to be an adulteress. To do so would have been to condemn her to a worse fate. To do so would have been to hate her. Rather, his actions told her, *Dear one, you were meant for so much more. Now be empowered by my faith, hope, and love and go live a sinless life.*

Love is not the denial of sin. It's not indifference toward what steals life and wholeness. That's tolerance, not love. Love hates anything that unmakes us.

That is why love is the proper response, God's response, to sin. Love patiently moves us toward freedom and wholeness. Love sets us free from sin's shame and power. Love works with us, going deep into the core of our being until we find ourselves aware of and alive to the fullness of salvation.

Tolerance runs from the tension. It's terrified of discomfort. "Hey, just do you!" it cries. Selfishness and fear are its friends. Championing a false authenticity, tolerance encourages its victims to stay in the shallowest of waters. It never encourages them toward the deeper currents of being.

But God can't do this. He won't do it. He calls to the deepest part of our self—the True Self—to know and be known. He says to us, *Take the plunge into my love. In it, you'll find patient endurance. I'll take you places you never thought you could go. I'll reshape you into the image of my Son. There you will find the rest and purpose your soul desires.*

## NAME-CALLING

Have you ever been called *Satan*? I don't know if I can think of a worse, more unloving insult.

Yet that is exactly what Jesus called Peter.

Peter—the man who left everything to follow Jesus. The man who would one day be crucified upside down. And you know what's wild? Just four *verses* before calling Peter Satan, Jesus prophesies that his church would be built on this man—the same Peter he's now calling Satan.

I've heard people try to downplay this incident. They need to keep up their nice guy image of Jesus, all smiles, healings, and free bread. But there's no getting around this one: "Get behind me, Satan! You are a hindrance to me. For you are not setting your mind on the things of God, but on the things of man" (Matt. 16:23).

So why was Jesus indignant? What had Peter done to provoke such a charged response? Let's take a look:

> From that time Jesus began to show his disciples that he must go to Jerusalem and suffer many things from the elders and chief priests and scribes, and be killed, and on the third day be raised. And Peter took him aside and began to rebuke him, saying, "Far be it from you, Lord! This shall never happen to you." (vv. 21–22)

On the surface, Peter's response to Jesus was full of love. After all, isn't it loving to not want someone to die? But if we look deeper, we find that Peter's words were rooted in fear—fear for his own life and calling. This wasn't real love. It was selfishness.

Jesus, on the other hand, responded in love *by calling Peter Satan.*

You see, Jesus understands better than any of us that we are all works in progress. When he corrects us, it isn't a form of rejection; rather, it's the confirmation of his vision for our lives and his belief in us. We are destined for more. We are capable of more. So he calls us onward toward that more. His seemingly harsh words were full of true love and void of pacifying niceties. Jesus was willing to die for Peter, so he had no problem telling him the truth.

In a similar way, God's confidence about what he's placed on and within us won't let him relent. His love won't let him compromise. Faithfully, he moves us forward.

This is the kind of love we should have for one another— the kind of love that is very different from the world's love.

It is a love of selfless devotion. A love that is willing to declare, "Things aren't right!"

Yes, there are "Christians" who supposedly take this approach. There are many who stand on the sidelines and point out what is wrong with the world. But these people always lack one thing: they are unwilling to die for the people they point their finger at. Their intensity and indignation spring from self-righteousness, not love.

There's a reason why after correcting Peter, Jesus immediately talks about the cost of following him. The cost of knowing his love and learning his ways. He says to his disciples:

> Whoever wants to be my disciple must deny themselves and take up their cross and follow me. For whoever wants to save their life[a] will lose it, but whoever loses their life for me will find it. What good will it be for someone to gain the whole world, yet forfeit their soul? Or what can anyone give in exchange for their soul? (vv. 24–26 NIV)

Since the ultimate act of love was the cross, taking up our crosses is the continuation and representation of that love. There's no way around it. Life is found only in death to the False Self. More specifically, we must die to self in the arms of Love. In these arms, we learn how to love others. Love them to the point at which we would die for them.

That is the goal of love. Like Jesus, we are to love the world so much that we are willing to die for it. "This is my commandment, that you love one another as I have loved you" (John 15:12). When we love like Jesus, we are willing to die to self, pretense, comfort, and anything else that keeps us from loving the way he loves. From this position of selfless love, we can cast aside tolerance and learn patient endurance.

## LOVING OUR WORLD

George MacDonald once wrote that God's "determination is that his sons and daughters shall love each other perfectly. He gave us to each other to belong to each other forever."[7] True love escapes the confines of time, belonging to an eternal story.

We don't love well when we view life only through a temporal lens. The reality is faith, hope, and love last forever. They will always be part of our lives. When we embrace their transcendent nature, we play by the rules and ways of heaven, opening our lives to the largeness of true love—the intimate and eternal sort.

True love will inevitably create tension in our world. It requires us to actually care for people. And caring for people creates conflict—it makes things messy. Too often we run from this conflict because we despise the tension it brings. We don't want to be peacemakers; we want to be peacekeepers. The status quo is too easy, too convenient. Why fight the system? Why be disruptive?

But Jesus's message was and is that the world's system— largely driven by its idea of love and relationships—is tragically flawed. It must be cast aside so something new can take its place. We must fight the system!

Tragically and ironically, the self-centered love of this world makes the self hopelessly small. That is why we, as the people of God, have to believe we are who God says we are: sons and daughters of the Most High, re-created in Christ and entrusted with a glorious message of reconciliation that extends beyond us (2 Cor. 5:18–19).

Most people don't truly love themselves—they love a False Self they undoubtedly know is unworthy of love. This spurning of themselves, even if it masquerades as self-love, will cause them to treat others with similar contempt, precluding real connection.

But true love will open your heart to others, giving you an intimate understanding of their fears, needs, and struggles. In this knowledge, you will be able to love them as you've learned to love yourself, your True Self—the one reborn in Life, vibrating with truth and overflowing with love.

Can you imagine a world where God's Saints pursue such a love—a world where our relationships are infused by his faith and hope? What a glorious world. We would spur one another onward in patient endurance. This is the love that would mark us as his. This is a holy love, a derivative of God's otherness. Such a love is worth chasing. Ultimately, this is the love that will mark the systems of God's new world.

I've seen glimpses of this love in my own marriage, family, and community. (But I want to see more.) This love creates unbreakable bonds of fraternity and trust. It forges an intimacy that is wildly beautiful. And it makes space for a growth that exceeds expectation and perceived limitation.

This kind of love loves unto perfection.

## PERFECTION

The word *perfection* often leaves a bad taste in our mouths. It can feel like a big tease. A goodie dangled on a string just beyond our outstretched fingers. A reminder that we're not good enough and never will be.

I'm a firstborn and a perfectionist. (Yes, I know that "perfectionist" is an oversimplification, but bear with me.) As a kid, I constantly felt like I was one sin away from hell . . . or from becoming the antichrist. My Christian experience passed through my lens of self, circumventing the whole idea of me being a new creation *in* Christ. And I could never be good enough for God.

But around my twenty-first birthday, everything changed. That summer—I'm a June baby—brought a revelation of love that has reshaped my life. I began to get a picture of how God sees me. And my idea of perfection started to change.

Fast-forward ten years. I'm still a perfectionist (just ask my wife), but I'm confident in who I am in Christ. And a revelation of God's love and commitment to me has set me free from being consumed with my own perfection, or lack thereof.

Now when I encounter areas of my life that are less-than-perfect (and there are a lot of them), I can humble myself and make room for God's grace to do what only it can do: redeem my past and empower my future. By not obsessing over my idea of perfection—and ardently defending that position—I am, ironically, moving toward a higher perfection. That's the power of humility.

This release of my idea of perfection—which is hopelessly smaller than God's plan for my wholeness—has set me free from the power of condemnation. In fact, I have not struggled with condemnation in over a decade. Yet at the same time, I've never been more keenly aware of the disconnect between where I am today and where God desires me to be. While I haven't known condemnation, I've had to get comfortable navigating the seas of conviction.

*+I+*

Too often conviction and condemnation are thrown into the same bucket, so I want to highlight a few of their major differences.

Conviction is painful, but there's hope. The pain is rooted in how our decisions affect God and others. Conviction is God- and others-centered. Ultimately, it attaches itself to an image or vision of where God is taking us—you could say it propels us forward.

Condemnation is painful, and there's no hope. The pain is primarily rooted in how our decisions have affected us. Condemnation is self-centered. Ultimately, it attaches itself to our past, a vision of who we have been. It makes us feel stuck, filling us with fear and keeping us from moving forward.

As you can see, pain comes with both conviction and condemnation. In other words, there's no escaping pain. And that's not a bad thing. Pain is good as long as it is necessary.

When we welcome God's ability to redeem pain, we journey toward true perfection. James unpacks this idea: "Count it all joy, my brothers, when you meet trials of various kinds, for you know that the testing of your faith produces steadfastness. And let steadfastness have its *full effect*, that you may be *perfect* and complete, lacking in nothing" (James 1:2–4, emphasis added).

Notice that James begins with a celebratory remark. Rejoice when you go through trials! Revel in your pain! At first glance, we have to wonder if James has lost his mind. Has the persecution gone to his head? But when we read on, we see that James couldn't be saner.

The Greek word *teleios* translated "full effect" and "perfect" is one of my favorite Greek words. We really don't have an English word that does it justice. It's not a perfection that comes from following all the rules or checking the boxes. It's a perfection or wholeness that comes only through a process. It's a perfection built on patience, faith, and dedication.

James's point is that God uses the trials (or pain) in our lives to purify us and make us whole. God doesn't waste anything. He even finds ways to redeem the pain and trials—caused by our own personal sins and the general brokenness of this world—to complete a perfect work in us. His love for us took on human form so that he might intimately lead us through the suffering. This is why the writer of Hebrews tells us that Jesus learned obedience through suffering and was made *perfect* (same root as *teleios*) through the process (5:8–9). It was through obedience in the process that Jesus "became truly and fully what in His nature He already was."[8]

We don't like the idea of suffering. But God uses the pain to reveal our new life, the True Self. When speaking of Paul, God said, "I will show him how much he must suffer for the sake of my name" (Acts 9:16). There's no malice in these words. Never have words been more full of love because everything God says and does is from a place of love. Even in and through judgment he loves us. God's love does not vacillate. He is always the same. He is the immutable God. Forever constant. Always good.

## FIERY LOVE

I want to end this chapter by heading back to 1 Corinthians 13.

> If I were to speak with eloquence in earth's many languages, and in the heavenly tongues of angels, yet I didn't express myself with *love*, my words would be reduced to the hollow sound of nothing more than a clanging cymbal. (v. 1 TPT, emphasis added)

I've used *The Passion Translation* here because it offers footnotes that explain some of the distinctions between the Greek and Aramaic texts of the New Testament. While the authoritative manuscripts are in Greek, I enjoy seeing some of the nuances found in the Aramaic texts.

The Aramaic word for love found in this verse is *hooba*, and it is a homonym that also means "to set on fire." The idea is that this love erupts from "the inner depths of the heart as an eternal energy, an active power of bonding hearts and lives in *secure relationships*."[9]

At the end of the day, love is about intimacy and relationship. We're all looking for this type of secure connection. The good life cannot be found without it. Relationships are what bind us together and give life its meaning. That's why God is so committed to helping us discover love and develop the capacity to love others well.

God sees us both as we are and how we should be. And he loves us everywhere in between. We can be confident in his love. In patience, we can welcome the pain of the process—even when it doesn't make sense. God promises to redeem the pain, weaving it together to reveal our True Self—secure in him. That's his vision for us—and it's a vision he was willing to die for.

If we welcome God's patient, fiery love—the love that loves unto purity—then we escape the bonds of our False Self and experience perfect wholeness. This perfection has already been spoken over us and given to us in Christ.

Full of faith, God is completely in love with you. True love cannot and will not be contained. Nothing can separate us from its power; space, time, and matter can't hold it down (Rom. 8:37–39). The perfect Lamb has overcome the limits of chronology. He is love. The question is, Will you dive into this fiery love? Will you be okay with not understanding the heights and depths and bounds of its reach?

Love has won. And God sees you in his victory.

## UNMADE

Shadows and shades.
Masks and memes.
Sameness is kindness.
The status quo supreme.

There's safety and chaos,
And rules in between.
Rules that make our lives small,
Predictable and clean.

But the Author of life
Is anything but safe.
His love is dangerous,
Savage his grace.

He desires the False Self—
That perversion of being.
Its death is your gift,
Your wonder's revealing.

Don't deny who you are.
Your True Self is calling.
The unmaking is now,
Charades are falling.

Nearby there's a dance called life,
Move toward its rhythm and song.
In this cadence of splendor,
You'll find you belong.

November 10, 2018
Colorado Springs

# BACK TO LIFE

*The First Man was made out of earth,*
*and people since then are earthy;*
*the Second Man was made out of heaven,*
*and people now can be heavenly.*
*In the same way that we've worked*
*from our earthy origins,*
*let's embrace our heavenly ends.*
*—1 Corinthians 15:47–49 MSG*

I n his book *The Song of the Bird*, Anthony de Mello tells the following story:

A man found an eagle's egg and put it in the nest of a barnyard hen. The eaglet hatched with the brood of chicks and grew up with them.

All his life the eagle did what the barnyard chicks did, thinking he was a barnyard chick. He scratched the earth for worms and insects, he clucked and cackled. And he would thrash his wings and fly a few feet into the air.

Years passed and the eagle grew very old. One day he saw a magnificent bird above him in the cloudless sky. It glided in graceful majesty among the powerful wind currents, with scarcely a beat of its strong golden wings. The eagle looked up in awe. "Who's that?" he asked.

"That's the eagle, the king of the birds," said his neighbor. "He belongs to the sky. We belong to the earth—we are chickens."

So the eagle lived and died a chicken, for that's what he thought he was.[1]

For the eagle to become what he was created to be, he would have had to unlearn much of what he knew about himself. In many ways, it was easier to remain a chicken. The chicken way was all he'd ever known. Being a chicken had its challenges—like not being able to get more than a few feet off the ground—but it was safe, familiar. And there was free food and shelter.

He couldn't be an eagle and a chicken. Sure, he could be an eagle that would, at times, forget what he was and let out a big cluck. But he couldn't be an eagle without joining the skies. After all, what is an eagle without his flight?

Likewise, it's not easy for us to unlearn something. Our brains make countless assumptions for the sake of efficiency. And these suppositions quickly turn into facts if left unchallenged. In a real sense, we become *inattentionally* blind, collecting data that only supports our existing assumptions about ourselves and our world.

Behaviors and preferences are built on what we believe—the conscious or subconscious "facts" that govern our lives.

It's hard to leave behind the familiar, the known, the quasi proven, especially when our identity, purpose, or pleasure is at stake. In our false humanity, we have created complex ideas of what it takes to be happy and fulfilled. Distracted, hungry, and disillusioned, we spend our lives chasing the familiar gods of sex, stuff, and status, often using religion as just another altar to worship them.

But we were made for higher things. We weren't destined to be slaves of temporal whims. After all, we're eternal beings—so only the eternal will satisfy our cravings.

In God's redemptive style, he uses our world's brokenness to seed us for what's to come. In other words, he uses temporal struggles to forge eternal beauty. This is why Paul writes:

> We are children of God, and if children, then heirs—heirs of God and fellow heirs with Christ, provided that we suffer with him in order that we may also be glorified with him.
>
> For I consider that the sufferings of this present time are not worth comparing with the glory that is to be revealed to us. For the creation waits with eager longing for the revealing of the [children] of God. (Rom. 8:16–19)

The sufferings of the present are not even worth comparing to the glory before us. And notice that these sufferings are inseparable from our new life in Christ. In fact, we cannot be sons and daughters of God without these growing pains. The world is not right. We are not right. And the pain is evidence of God's Spirit lovingly guiding us toward freedom and wholeness. These pains bring the futility of the False Self into focus and position us to welcome the Spirit's life, which can fill the depths of our immortal souls.

All of creation is longing for us to realize the mystery of Christ in us, the hope of glory. We've been content to play religion—making a god in our own image—when God is calling us onto the waters of new creation. The question is,

Are we willing to yield to our new life in Christ, or are we going to just put some nice church clothes on the Old Self?

Often we look at hardships as God trying to teach us something. But more often than not, God uses trials to help us unlearn what unmakes us. Trials offer a divorce from pride's foolishness—they invite us to return to our childlike state. That state of being that is simultaneously full of confidence and humility. That state of being that can enter God's kingdom: "Truly, I say to you, unless you turn and become like children, you will never enter the kingdom of heaven" (Matt. 18:3). Without becoming childlike, we cannot know the simplicity and the sincerity of the good life.

If we are to find the good life, there's so much we have to unlearn, starting with our identity. That is why the ideas of God's kingdom, life, and salvation are often accompanied by metaphors involving rebirth. In order for us to receive the newness of the life found in God, we have to become someone new. Children are new creations; they are, in a sense, blank canvases, ready for whatever brushstrokes may come.

In fact, babies are born with only two fears: loud noises and falling.[2] I think the kingdom of God requires childlikeness because it's a terrifying, seemingly impossible new way to be human. And if we are to make the jump into new life, we'll need to unlearn the old fears and "facts" that make our lives small.

The question is, Will we be people of the flesh or people of the Spirit?

Resurrection life compels us to look upward and spread our wings. If we happen to cluck, God's not going to cast us from the skies. He will, however, remind us that we were created to soar.

## HOLINESS OF LIFE

> It's resurrection, resurrection, always resurrection, that undergirds what I do and say, the way I live. . . . Think straight. Awaken to the holiness of life. (1 Cor. 15:30–34 MSG)

I love the way *The Message* paraphrase links resurrection with the holiness of life. As we know, holiness is not just following the rules; rather, it is a life marked by God's otherness—*the* quality that makes him God. As God's children, we are to run toward the promise of holiness, casting aside anything that distorts our wholeness in Christ. If we are to experience new life—resurrection life—we have no other choice but to pursue holiness.

With Jesus's resurrection came a new way to be human—otherwise, we wouldn't be able to awaken to the holiness of life. But in Jesus, we find a new life that should be known now and experienced in full upon his return. The new life that is available to us now is proof of both his resurrection *and* his promised return.

Second Corinthians 5:17 can be literally translated, "Therefore, if anyone is in Christ, there is a new created order. The old has passed away, behold, the new has come." There is (not "will be") a new created order, and the old has passed away (not "will pass away") and the new has come (not "will come").

"Of his own will," writes James, "he brought us forth by the word of truth, that we should be a kind of firstfruits of his creatures" (James 1:18). God's Saints are the firstfruits of what's to come. We're evidence of the power of the cross, and we point toward the new creation reality of the promised day. We work for and toward that future reality, faithfully dying to our False Self so that we may know Jesus's resurrection life, the life that is already available through his Spirit within us.

In both 2 Corinthians and Ephesians, Paul uses an engagement ring metaphor to convey the peculiar relationship between our new life now and the promised life to come.

When two people get engaged, things change. It's no longer "that's my girlfriend"; it's now "that's my fiancée." There's an implicit promise that comes with the label.

I remember the first time I referred to Julianna as my girlfriend after I had proposed to her. I got a dirty look. Things had changed—Juli now had a ring on her finger. She didn't like my reducing our relationship to mere boyfriend/girlfriend status.

We had made a commitment to each other, and our lives were consumed with moving toward our promised wedding date. Our wedding was the promise—it was the goal. And in order to speed up our journey toward that promise, we made many decisions and sacrifices that brought us closer and closer to our promised reality.

We started living and acting differently. There was money to be saved. An apartment to be found. Premarital counseling to be had. Relationships to adjust (got to love those in-laws). Habits to be developed. Work to be done.

These intentional efforts were driven by two things.

First, the security of our new relational status. With our engagement came a confidence and an assurance that energized and fueled the process. We were willing to do the hard things because we had a preliminary "yes" that made us believe we'd hear "I do" at the altar.

Second, our promised wedding date. "We're getting married on October 25" was the hope we needed when things got difficult. That date brought everything into focus and reminded us that the engagement season was only temporary. Eventually, the glorious day would come, and we would become one, journeying into new levels of intimacy and togetherness.

If you've navigated engagement, you know how awkward that season can be. People romanticize the waiting and planning process, but it's not all shopping for dresses and tasting cakes. It's hard work. Not to mention, there's the tremendous sexual tension when you're waiting until after your wedding to have sex.

With an engagement comes both great excitement and frustration. I've heard many couples say, "We just wish our wedding day was here! Things would be so much better!" It's not that their lives are terrible, but they feel like they may explode from all the hope and excitement.

When we are joined to Christ, filled with his new life, in a real sense, we welcome both excitement and frustration. Excitement over our promised new life and the glimpses of that new life now. And frustration that we cannot fully know as we are known. Frustration that we have not yet known unhindered intimacy and wholeness. Frustration that our world is still broken and there's tremendous work to be done.

Here's the thing: when you really explore your new life in Christ, you will find yourself more whole, more satisfied, and yet, at the same time, more full of anticipation—a longing that's deeper than anything you could have ever imagined. And that's okay. It is in the longing that our souls expand, making room for the greatest of loves.

## DEATH TO SELF

When we are joined to Christ, we are given freedom from the old life or the False Self. But just as a bride can reject her groom, so we can reject our new life in Christ. Yes, even after receiving the promise of new life, we can choose to go back to our old ways. Rather than making Jesus the Lord and love of our lives, we can choose to worship our first lord and love: self. This is why Jesus continually told us to deny ourselves if we want to follow in his footsteps and experience his new life.

There's no getting around it—self must be sacrificed if resurrection life is to be found. So the question is, How do we sacrifice self?

Almost every major religion recognizes the need for a death to a False Self. What makes Christianity different is that we find a New Self not through our own enlightenment or moral effort but through a willingness to lose our lives in Christ, exchanging our False Self for a True Self re-created in his likeness and animated by his Spirit. Paul tells us:

I have been crucified with Christ. It is no longer I who live, but Christ who lives in me. And the life I now live in the flesh I live by faith in the Son of God, who loved me and gave himself for me. (Gal. 2:20)

We know that our old self was crucified with him in order that the body of sin might be brought to nothing. . . . For one who has died has been set free from sin. Now if we have died with Christ, we believe that we will also live with him. (Rom. 6:6–8)

Sin, which we know finds its strength in self-worship, is what keeps us from enjoying resurrection life. Please don't revert to the old way of viewing sin as the mere breaking of rules. Sin is what steals life because it puts something other than God and his will on the throne of our lives. When we died with Christ, we were set free from sin's power. I realize that may seem like an impossible statement, but it is true. Either we believe it is true, or we must diminish the potency of the cross.

Every day, every hour, every moment, we have a choice. We can choose to align ourselves with our promised new life, leaning into the tension that comes with that hope, or we can live in the vapidity of our False Self, chasing the gods of this world. There's a reason Jesus said to take up our crosses *daily* (Luke 9:23). Paul echoes this sentiment in 1 Corinthians 15—a chapter all about resurrection life.

Our journey toward wholeness in Christ is like traveling through an onion—there's layer upon layer. And with each breakthrough comes a greater awareness of the largeness of our freedom. Whether we're just starting this journey or we've been on it for years, progress requires the same thing: death to self. And when we die to self, we escape the bonds of sin's smallness.

Paul makes it clear that we will not enjoy our new life if we continue to obey the desires of our False Self: "Do you not know that if you present yourselves to anyone as obedient slaves, you are slaves of the one whom you obey, either of sin, which leads to death, or of obedience, which leads to righteousness?" (Rom. 6:16).

But we have a choice. Paul continues:

> For just as you once presented your members as slaves to impurity and to lawlessness leading to more lawlessness, so now present your members as slaves to righteousness leading to sanctification. . . . Now that you have been set free from sin and have become slaves of God, the fruit you get leads to sanctification and its end, eternal life. (vv. 19, 22)

Sanctification—which is just another way of describing our yielding to Christ's saving power—is the journey to wholeness. It's the process of unpacking and discovering the fullness and wonder of the gift of salvation. Paul makes it clear that sanctification's destination is not religious elitism or snobby asceticism. Rather, sanctification's aim is the beauty and perfection of eternal life. The life that will always be the cry of our souls.

And here's the truth: you can experience as much of that life now as you are willing to have. God is not trying to hold that life back from you. He wants to give it to you. But there is a cost—surrender. More specifically, you have to surrender your understanding of your identity. Not because God wants faceless children—nothing could be further from the truth. You must surrender your identity—the life you have now—so that you can gain eyes to see yourself the way God sees you: as his child, reflecting his nature. "We are God's children now, and what we will be has not yet appeared; but we know that when he appears we shall be like him, because we shall see him as he is. And everyone who thus hopes in him purifies himself as he is pure" (1 John 3:2–3).

Do you see the tension between who we are and who we will be? We are his children now, but what this means is a mystery in many ways: The promise, however, is that we can journey further up and further in to that mystery and become more and more what we already are.

The day will come when we will see Jesus as he truly is. There will be no shroud to hide his beauty. And in that moment, we will know him as we are known. But we don't have to be passive in our hope or dull in our waiting. Because God's Spirit lives in us ("we are God's children now"), we can actively pursue this hope, and even now, by his Spirit, we can catch enough glimpses of his glory to shake up our world.

Today, right now, we are his offspring—his seed and Spirit are in us. And because we have this new nature, we can know the ways of our Father: peace, joy, love, righteousness, justice, and more. But we cannot know this new creation reality if we refuse to reject the sin, selfishness, and smallness that's native to our False Self.

## THE FREEDOM OF GRACE

In one of his letters to Timothy, Paul describes what we become when we reject our new nature in Christ. He offers a list of symptoms that will escalate as time is rolled up and this age comes to an end. Keep in mind that this list is not referring to "lost" people. Rather, Paul is explicitly describing Christians who deny God's power to redeem and regenerate their lives in the present.

> For people will be lovers of self, lovers of money, proud, arrogant, abusive, disobedient to their parents, ungrateful, unholy, heartless, unappeasable, slanderous, without self-control, brutal, not loving good, treacherous, reckless, swollen with conceit, lovers of pleasure rather than lovers of God, having the appearance of godliness, but denying its power. (2 Tim. 3:2–5)

Notice that the first symptom is *lovers of self.* These "Christians" will hold fast to their False Self. They'll claim to be children of God but deny grace's power to transform their lives. They may say some of the right things, but their actions will reveal who is actually lord of their lives—self.

Peter and Jude describe these people as those who pervert grace for their own sakes (2 Pet. 3:14–18; Jude 4).

Grace never encourages or perpetuates our false, sinful humanity. Grace is the radical divine power that sets us free from both sin's penalty and sin's power, positioning us to know our new life in Christ. Our misunderstanding of grace is one of the primary reasons we do not find the power to let go of the False Self. "God's grace [*charis*] includes favor and supernatural potency, and it is meant to leave us both charming and beautiful. In classical Greek it was meant to convey the attitude of favor shown by royalty."[3]

We must stop cheapening grace, using it merely as a cover-up for our sins. Cheap grace is cut-rate forgiveness, cut-rate comfort—it is grace without a price. Dietrich Bonhoeffer, the German pastor who resisted the Nazi regime, wrote:

> Costly grace is the gospel. . . . It is costly, because it calls to discipleship; it is grace, because it calls us to follow Jesus Christ. It is costly, because it costs people their lives; it is grace, because it gives people their lives. It is costly, because it condemns sin; it is grace, because it justifies the sinner.[4]

## IT'S NOT JUST FOR US

Resurrection life is ultimately about freedom. Freedom from anything that unmakes us, from the fears and pride that feed sin and bolster our false humanity. And freedom to become God's children, reflecting his holiness and righteousness to our world.

You see, our new life isn't just about us. Yes, it moves in and through us, reshaping us. But it doesn't stop there. We are re-created in Christ to be a conduit of his life so that others might follow us into the arms of the Father. We are most alive when we are channeling God's grace, love, and holiness.

But God's Saints are not supposed to be mere spectacles—pseudogods worshiped by lower life-forms. The early disciples were mistaken as gods, and nothing made them more upset. Look at how Barnabas and Paul responded when they were called Zeus and Hermes:

> When the apostles Barnabas and Paul heard of it, they tore their garments and rushed out into the crowd, crying out, "Men, why are you doing these things? We also are men, of like nature with you, and we bring you good news, that you should turn from these vain things to a living God." (Acts 14:14–15)

However, as our new life, and everything that comes with it, reveals the only true way to be human, this should cause people to look on us with awe. After all, we are supposed to reflect God's glory. The glory is not ours, but as we grow in Christ, we should reflect more and more of who God is.

God doesn't hate our humanity. He loves it. He became a man so we could spend eternity following in the steps of the perfect man. And by the Spirit of Christ in us, we can begin taking those steps now and invite others to join the journey.

We don't start living until we discover something worth dying for. Jesus picked up his cross for the sake of the world. Are you willing to die to yourself for the sake of your world?

As we saw in the last chapter, death to self does not translate to instant perfection. This is a daily journey, each day offering a greater revelation of the wholeness God is moving us toward. But we must start somewhere, moving forward one step at a time.

## BEYOND YOU

Peter offers a good example for us to follow. We make jokes about him sinking in the waves, but at least he was out of the boat (Matt. 14:28–31). As you step into your new life, you will make mistakes. You'll miss the mark. Allow Peter's bravery and failure to infuse you with courage. Don't let fear keep you from stepping onto the waters of new creation.

We all know Peter started to sink because of doubt. But why did he doubt? Had he not seen Jesus do miraculous things? I don't think Peter doubted Jesus's power. Earlier that day he had watched Jesus feed thousands with just a few fish and loaves. No, Peter didn't doubt Jesus or his power. But he did doubt himself. He doubted whether he was worthy of such power. He became self-focused as opposed to God-centered.

The truth is your new life doesn't come from you, so don't make it about you. Frankly, it's about you simply getting over yourself so you can be found in Christ. But it's not easy to get over yourself. That's why the hardest thing to lay down at the cross is our opinion of ourselves.

We see in Scripture that Peter went through quite the process to get over himself. There was the embarrassment of being called Satan (Matt. 16:23), the foolishness on the mount of transfiguration (Luke 9:33), the denying of Jesus three times (John 18:15–27), the rebuke from Paul regarding his hypocrisy (Gal. 2:11–14), and the painful conversation with Jesus (John 21:15–22). But eventually we find Peter so free from self's tyranny that he volunteers to be crucified upside down—simply because he didn't want the honor that came with dying in the same manner as his Savior.

If God used this imperfect man to build his church, why wouldn't he use us to reveal the wonders of our new life in Christ?

Sure, you will cluck like a chicken at times—Peter certainly did—but that doesn't make you a chicken. When you start acting like a chicken, remind yourself of Christ's vision for you and, by the Spirit of grace, start flapping your wings and head toward the skies of higher living.

## THE IN-BETWEEN

From an anatomical and biochemical standpoint, we remain broken in many ways. Our bodies and their systems are subject to decay. Every day, we move closer to our physical death. It's foolish for us to deny the challenges that come with our brokenness. But here's the good news: God can and does do miracles. When Paul writes in Romans 8:11 that "the Spirit . . . who raised Christ Jesus from the dead will also give life to your mortal bodies through his Spirit who dwells in you," he's alluding to both a current and a future state of being. Although we do not have our resurrected bodies now, we can experience resurrection life by the power of God's Spirit—the same Spirit who will give life to our resurrected, imperishable bodies.

"One of our great woes," writes A. W. Tozer, "is the constant warfare between the eternity in our hearts and the time in our bodies."[5] It's easy for us to see our progress, or lack thereof, and think, *Why bother, there's no way I will ever become a Saint.* But here's the truth: with every act of obedient surrender, you become more whole.

It's normal for us to experience various measures of discouragement as we encounter the baser parts of our humanity. Most of us will use distraction or pleasure or busyness to keep those parts of us hidden. But real growth invites us to confront the depths of our brokenness through the power of humility and grace. With every humble step, we tear down our False Self and make space for the transforming power of grace.

You may believe you are incapable of such growth, such wondrous new life, but growth follows obedience. And the ultimate act of obedience is to believe and receive what God says about us in his Word. Before we can live the Christian life, we must believe we're empowered to be Saints. So take the next step of obedience, however small it may be. By doing so, you will find greater capacity to obey. The capacity to obey always follows obedience. That may seem nonsensical, but it's how God works. Try it and you will see.

## THE JOURNEY HOME

The Spirit intends to investigate our whole life history, layer by layer, throwing out the junk and preserving the values that were appropriate to each stage of our human development. . . . Eventually the Spirit begins to dig into the bedrock of our earliest emotional life. . . . Hence, as we progress toward the center where God actually is waiting for us, we are naturally going to feel that we are getting worse. This warns us that the spiritual journey is not a success story or a career move. It is rather a series of humiliations of the false self.[6]

This "series of humiliations" is no fun, but it's the pathway of grace. It's the pathway toward our new life in Christ.

Your obedience and surrender create the conditions for your new life to break forth. Wholeness is already yours, despite what you may not see. Jesus was broken to make you whole. Because of this, you don't have to fear allowing his Spirit to break down your facades and reveal your True Self.

Our new life in Christ is the treasure in the field that's worth selling everything to buy (Matt. 13:44); it's the identity energized by God's eternal kingdom. The question is, Will we let go of everything to have the one thing worth having? When we surrender, we create the conditions for the seed inside of us to spring to life and become something new.

> The kingdom of heaven is like a grain of mustard seed that a man took and sowed in his field. It is the smallest of all seeds, but when it has grown it is larger than all the garden plants and becomes a tree, so that the birds of the air come and make nests in its branches. (Matt. 13:31–32)

When Jesus speaks of faith and the mustard seed, he's describing what seems like an impossible change. How could a little seed become such a large tree—a tree that provides refuge and support to others? But this is the power of God's kingdom reality. Though it may initially seem small in our lives, it will grow into something beautiful, spacious, and practical.

Through faith, the Old Self—that giant mountain that's been built on years of labels, limiting beliefs, and lies—can be thrown into the ocean. The True Self, our new creation reality in Christ that may now seem as small as a mustard seed, will overcome the old and reveal the new.

Take a step toward surrender and watch God's grace show up. Suddenly, you'll find yourself able to forgive those who seemed beyond your ability to love. You'll have joy to share with those in despair. You'll know freedom from the labels society worships. With Paul, you'll declare, "There is neither Jew nor Greek, there is neither slave nor free, there is no male and female, for [we] are all one in Christ Jesus" (Gal. 3:28).

In beauty, you'll stand confident in a faceless world. But first, you must find your True Self through obedient surrender—you must take up your cross.

In many ways, this process of transformation feels like walking toward a massive mountain, far in the distance. Depending on the terrain, there are moments when the mountain seems to be getting farther away. When this happens, it's tempting to convince ourselves we're traveling backward, away from our promised True Self. But that is not the case. With every step, we are getting closer—despite what our eyes may tell us. The good life is that mountain. Its beauty and enormity beckon us. The mountain reminds us that the flatland is not all there is. There *is* a place that reaches into the heavens. Although it may seem foreign, we know it is home.

# GLORY

*The mystery hidden for ages and generations*
*but now revealed to his saints.*
*To them God chose to make known . . .*
*the riches of the glory of this mystery,*
*which is Christ in you, the hope of glory.*
*—Colossians 1:26–27*

We were made for glory. That's why we
strive and toil, searching for that something more. It's why we scrape and
scratch for the good life. It's why we
add layer upon layer to the False Self. There's a crater in our
being, an impression left by the breath of God. Its largeness
terrifies us, so we'll do anything to fill the hole. But this hole
cannot be filled by the gods of this world and their prizes of
splendor. This space must be occupied by its Maker. Only
God's glory can fill our souls.

We were made for glory.

But what does this glory look like? How does it feel?
Is it a new and improved version of the world's glory—a
striking coalescence of fame, power, and grandeur? Or is
it something *other* than what we've seen?

In Mark 10, we find two brothers who want a piece of glory. James and John, the sons of thunder, are movers and shakers; they are members of Jesus's most inner circle. They've seen and participated in the miraculous. They can feel the scales of power tipping in their direction. More and more people are following Jesus. The streets are buzzing with whispers that there's a messiah in town—a man who will defeat Caesar's kingdom and establish his own.

These brothers realize that the impending shift in power will offer new opportunities, specifically, grand positions of authority. And with authority comes glory. They want in on this new glory and decide to act swiftly. Trying not to alert the other disciples, they surreptitiously pull Jesus aside to procure their positions of prominence. Their request has significant implications, and since fortune favors only the bold, they don't hold back, hoping their initiative and audacity will earn them a favorable response: "Teacher, we want you to do for us whatever we ask of you" (v. 35).

What nerve. They're trying to bully the Son of God into giving them a blank check. "Trust us—you'll want to sign off on this idea." These really are sons of thunder. Maybe Jesus should grant them whatever they ask. After all, he does seem rather fond of boldness.

Let's see how Jesus responds: "What do you want me to do for you?" (v. 36).

Notice that Jesus doesn't give them carte blanche; rather, he cuts through their smoke and mirrors. He certainly won't give them whatever they want, but he will hear them out. With excitement and some trepidation, James and John reply, "Grant us to sit, one at your right hand and one at your left, *in your glory*" (v. 37, emphasis added).

You have to give it to them. At least they're honest. They want the glory and everything that comes with it. They're swinging for the fences on the first pitch. The problem is their form is suspect. They're looking for glory in all the wrong places. So Jesus responds, "You do not know what you are asking" (v. 38). In other words, James and John don't know the first thing about his glory. Jesus continues, "To sit at my right hand or at my left is not mine to grant, but it is for those for whom it has been prepared" (v. 40).

Ouch. The sons of thunder are rejected. And to add insult to injury, the other disciples catch wind of their scheme and call them out. Peter and Andrew quickly plan their countermove. Everyone is indignant. *How dare James and John do such a thing!* But truthfully, they're all just upset they didn't think of it first. After all, Jesus has only one right and one left—two spots of ultimate glory—but there are twelve disciples. The math doesn't work. People are getting the shaft.

＋I＋

Let's fast-forward five chapters to Mark 15:25–27: "It was the third hour when they crucified him. And the inscription of the charge against him read, 'The King of the Jews.' And with him they crucified two robbers, *one on his right and one on his left*" (emphasis added).

Here we find the grand, public announcement of Jesus's kingdom. At last, the kingdom of this world (Rome) is siding with truth. The King of the Jews is lifted high for all to see. And in this moment of grotesque glory, we find two robbers by Jesus's side, "one on his right and one on his left." It is now clear that these criminals—rejected by society—are the ones Jesus alludes to in Mark 10. They are the ones who get to be by his side in this moment of triumph; they are the ones "for whom it has been prepared." It's painfully apparent to us, but not yet to the disciples, that Jesus's crucifixion is the moment when he is "in his glory."[1]

I'm sure James and John had a different type of glory in mind. They had witnessed the glory of Rome, the glory of the temple. They expected a glory like what they had known. Obviously, something greater than what they'd seen but, at the same time, similar. Something familiar. A perfected normal glory, if you will. But God's glory doesn't work like that. It's a majestic, physical presentation of his holiness that is visible to human sight.[2] In other words, where there's a physical presentation of his glory, we catch a glimpse of his holiness (or otherness). We catch a glimpse of the divine—the beauty of his majesty.

Jesus's death doesn't fit within our paradigm of glory. There is a crown, but its jewels are thorns. There is a banner of rulership, but its words are a jest. There is a robe, but its purpose is to shame.

None of this seems right. How is this a moment of glory?

✦ I ✦

What is so radical about the cross is its ability to redefine being and reframe the good life. The cross set the stage for a new way of being—a new type of glory. The glory we were made for. A glory found only in the largeness of losing one's life. Jesus had made this clear to them (and us) after James and John asked him for their seats of honor, but they didn't have ears to hear. Let's go back to Mark 10:

> You know that those who are considered rulers . . . lord it over them. . . . But it shall not be so among you. . . . Whoever would be first among you must be slave of all. For even the Son of Man came not to be served but to serve, and to give his life as a ransom for many. (vv. 42–45)

John's account also points to the moment of glory:

> The hour has come for the Son of Man to be *glorified*. Truly, truly I say to you, unless a grain of wheat falls into the earth and dies, it remains alone; but if it dies, it bears much fruit. Whoever loves his life loses it. . . . For this purpose I have come to this hour. Father, *glorify* your name. (John 12:23–25, 27–28, emphasis added)

Is there any question what hour Jesus is alluding to? This hour of glory is his crucifixion. It's the moment when Jesus glorifies his Father's name, revealing a new, eternal glory. "There are no crown-wearers in heaven who were not cross-bearers here below."[3]

I love how Jesus mentions the idea of the single grain of wheat (him) going into the ground. Jesus was and is God's only begotten Son. But because, in glory, he died and went into the ground, we, through the new life of his Spirit, can become partakers of his glory, reflecting his image, so that "he might be the firstborn among many" (Rom. 8:29). All of creation has been awaiting this redemption—this restoration of our Genesis mandate to be wise stewards of God's good creation.

✦─I─✦

James and John wanted significance for the sake of status. But that's not the way of the kingdom. Since the beginning of time, God has used his significance to serve us. Even to the point of death on a cross.

Jesus's life wasn't—in the conventional sense—glorious. He didn't even know where he would lay his head at night (Luke 9:58). Jesus seemed to travel aimlessly from one region to another, responding haphazardly to the needs around him. He was "uneducated" and from a region that failed to produce anything of worth. Yes, there were signs and wonders—miracles that turned some heads. But their wonder could be rationalized by intelligent folk, easily dismissed as fraudulent or the work of devils.

If Jesus was looking for conventional glory, it would have made more sense for him to be born into Caesar's family, becoming heir apparent of the greatest kingdom on earth. That would have given him unlimited access to the best poets, architects, artists, scholars, philosophers, rulers, and generals of his day. His influence would have been unparalleled. With so much status, he could have mandated and manipulated change through the most connected empire ever. But that's not what he did.

You see, Jesus's goal wasn't to make an empire for himself. He has always been about the kingdom. A new type of kingdom. A kingdom of kings and priests. He is the King of kings and the High Priest. We are the kings and queens that make him the King of kings. We are the priests, serving under the High Priest. (He wouldn't need the descriptor *High* if he were the only priest.) My point is Jesus is the greatest ruler because he multiplies his glory. And this multiplied glory was made possible by the unthinkable—the King of the world, the Author of life, surrendered to death. He welcomed grotesque glory so that we might become kings and queens—Saints who can share in his glory by receiving the breath of his new life.

Jesus couldn't come as Caesar because he was creating a new type of kingdom, a new type of rulership. Caesar lorded and paraded his glory, living aloof from his people. But Jesus, through his suffering and the giving of himself, reveals that he is truly all in all. Every bit matters to him. No person or sparrow is beyond his compassion. His Spirit hovers over all creation, working in us, preparing us for eternal glory.

That's why glory isn't found only in the high places; it's also in the day-to-day, the seemingly mundane or insignificant. Again, look at Jesus's life. He was a tradesman and could be mistaken for a homeless nomad. The point is he did normal life. Pilate and Herod were in their palaces; Jesus slept in the fields. But life happens in the fields. Crops are grown in the dust. From dust we come and to dust we go. Agriculture was the industry of his day, so Jesus went where the majority of people literally got their bread.

In many ways, Jesus's life was quite ordinary. He enjoyed meals, made witty remarks, constructed tables, played with kids, cried when friends died, paid his taxes. For thirty years, he lived in obscurity, and after just a few years of "ministry," he was sentenced to die outside the city of peace.

Abandoned to die on the cross.

## SHAME REDEFINED

The cross was a weapon of shame—the antithesis of glory. Rome was the most glorious empire in the world—the epitome of progress and culture. With such greatness to uphold, it had to humiliate and eradicate anyone who could compromise its glory. So the Romans used the cross—the ultimate tool of shame and death—to preserve Rome's splendor. The cross quickly became a public spectacle, a reminder of who was in charge. Its message: don't mess with Rome.

But Jesus flipped the script. Now, a couple millennia later, the cross is used as a symbol for life, purpose, and meaning. In the cross, we find the paradox of life in death, gain in sacrifice, glory in shame. Jesus unmasked the greatest empire, exposing its futility and emptiness. On Golgotha, the kingdom of heaven undermined the great Caesar, leaving Rome confounded: "Truly this was the Son of God!" (Matt. 27:54).

Why did this happen? Was it just the miracles? I don't think so. There have been many miracle workers over the years. Was it the teaching? There have been many great teachers.

Jesus astounded his world because he was in full what others were in part. And what really takes him over the edge, if you will—what makes him so complete—was (and is) the glory found in his self-sacrificial love. He modeled the love and glory that will mark the age to come—the promised heaven on earth. That day we will unlearn the ways of war and turn our weapons into tools for service. That day the lion and the lamb will lie down together. What glory will be found when we embrace Jesus's words: "You shall love the Lord your God with all your heart and with all your soul and with all your mind. This is the great and first commandment. And a second is like it: You shall love your neighbor as yourself. On these two commandments depend all the Law and the Prophets" (Matt. 22:37–40).

The law and the prophets were given to us so that we might find life. They were always signposts to something greater. This was the big idea on the mount of transfiguration. For a moment, Moses (the law), Elijah (the prophet), and Jesus (the Messiah) shared the mountain. But then a voice from heaven distinguished Jesus from the others. Suddenly, the law and the prophet vanished. Only the Messiah remained (Luke 9:35–36). In him, we find the peculiar, otherworldly glory that the law and the prophets always pointed toward.

I know it may seem cliché—a glory found in love and self-sacrifice—but isn't this what we crave? We are profoundly moved by accounts of selflessness. When was the last time you heard an audience shout for joy over a brilliant display of selfish glory? It just doesn't happen. There's something deep within us that harmonizes with God's otherness when we hear and feel the call to lay down our lives.

The challenge is we have been conditioned "to get ours," to take and not be taken from. But no matter what we do, there will always be someone who can and will take advantage of us. We can stick it to only so many people. Being the biggest and baddest is not a pathway to safety. It's isolating and exhausting. Glory is not found in being the greatest. It's in being the least of these, the servant of all. There's no glory without sacrifice. The old "look at how high and big I can build it" narrative should have been played out long ago.

Yes, we were made for glory. That's why we strive for significance. And that's not a bad thing. God wants us to stand out from the crowd. But we will not stand out if we become like the world, chasing its idea of glory. That's what everyone else does. Such a life is boorish and pathetic.

Regardless of where we live, what culture we grew up in, what socioeconomic class we belong to, we all have the opportunity to find glory by laying down our lives. Every day, every hour, every minute is pregnant with glory. But first we must get over ourselves and our illusions of depersonalized grandeur and see the world around us as it truly is. The world as it is today.

Your neighbors, classmates, coworkers, friends, and family have been entrusted to you. The brilliance of their lives is a reflection of your light. I don't say that to condemn you for your distraction, indifference, or inaction. I say that to inspire you. God has positioned you to share in his glory because that is your destiny. Any other pursuit will leave you frustrated and disillusioned.

I know this truth is hard. Most of us spend a lifetime before we learn how to live. In the face of death, we find clarity. You've probably seen this truth in the eyes of a dying loved one. Someone who wished they had more time. Someone who wished they had lived differently. Memories of missed risks and damaged relationships take on new forms. There's a lucidity that comes only with death. So God invites us to die now. Die to selfish ambition. Die to purposeless living. Die to small thinking. Die to sin's power. Why? So that we might know what it is to truly be alive, to participate in the mystery of life—that good life we all crave.

In Christ, death is not a thief of the future; it is a gift of the present.

## GRACE AND GLORY

Christ died in glory so that we could live in glory. That is the message of the cross. Jesus's cry "It is finished!" is the announcement of a glorious new way to be human. Love, life, and death were redefined on the cross. Stewardship, purpose, and identity were given new meaning. A great mystery unfolded before our eyes. And the floodgates of grace burst open, watering the seed of our new life in Christ.

Glory is our inheritance. It is the expression of God's otherness, brought to life within us by the power of his Spirit. But we won't step into this glory if we refuse to mature in our understanding of grace. These Saints put it well:

Grace is but glory begun, and glory is but grace perfected.

Jonathan Edwards[4]

Grace is nothing else than a beginning of glory in us.

Thomas Aquinas[5]

Grace leads to glory because it has the power to kill the False Self. The beauty of grace is that it reveals who we truly are by eliminating what we are not. In and through grace, our identity is found—whole, authentic, perfect, glorious. And this glory is not merely metaphysical, with no bearing on the here and now. Grace's purpose requires it to invade our very real lives—to intermingle with this dimension of time, space, and matter. It works in both the current and the prophetic, merging the worlds of what is and what will be. By doing so, grace brings us into the arms of our True Self, the self we've always known we were meant to be but could never find on our own.

What grace offers can be found nowhere else. Where it takes us is beyond the reach of self-help. Grace makes a mockery of self-help—it insults the idea that God is simply in the business of making us a slightly better version of ourselves. Grace is for glory—the glory of our King's holiness.

"The Son of Man came not to be served but to serve, and to give his life as a ransom for many" (Mark 10:45). This is Jesus's glory. The death that only he could give. But because of his death and new life, we can join in the mystery of the cross. We can find and know glory by losing our lives.

I love how the author of Hebrews weaves the themes of glory and grace:

> But we see him who for a little while was made lower than the angels, namely Jesus, crowned with glory and honor because of the suffering of death, so that by the grace of God he might taste death for everyone.
>
> For it was fitting that he, for whom and by whom all things exist, in bringing many sons [and daughters] to glory, should make the founder of their salvation perfect through suffering. For he who sanctifies and those who are sanctified all have one source. That is why he is not ashamed to call them brothers [and sisters]. (2:9–11)

It was the grace of God that led Jesus to his death—the very moment that was crowned with "glory and honor." It was grace that sustained him while blood leaked from his pores onto the grass in Gethsemane. It was grace that tended wounds from the lashes he received. It was grace that made holes in his hands so that we might become holy. It was by grace that he tasted death for everyone. And now it is by grace that we can follow in his footsteps and die to self, becoming sons and daughters of glory.

May we never get over amazing grace. It is the hope of our present and our future—merging what is and what will be. It is the breath of God, opening our lungs to the winds of new creation. By grace, we can lift our eyes and awaken the dawn.

We were made for glory.

Glory is the tune and rhythm of our life song. With the psalmist, our hearts cry, "Awake, my glory! Awake, O harp and lyre! I will awake the dawn!" (Ps. 57:8). We're living in the dawn of humanity and in the shadow of Jesus's new life. His grace has become our glory. His resurrection, our new life. And this new life is pregnant with purpose—a purpose much bigger than the smallness of selfishness. A purpose that invigorates each relationship, vocation, school, church, city—no matter how big or small—with an eternal glory. May we open our eyes to the reality of the final day. May we become people who practice and participate in the mystery of God's sovereign rule. May we become Saints, people of his otherness, children of his glory.

✦✝✦

The author of Hebrews implores us not to lose sight of our hope, the promise of a new life in Christ: "We are his house if indeed we hold fast our confidence and our boasting in our hope" (3:6). There's something outlandish here, something controversial. We are his house. The evidence of his genius. We are seen; he is unseen. But don't get it twisted—a house's brilliance is the reflection of its builder. He, Jesus, is the master builder. Every bit of "our glory" reflects him.

I know an amazing home builder here in Colorado Springs. He's won countless awards and is considered by many to be the best builder in the state. He once gave me a tour of one of his homes. It was an open house, and many people were perusing his masterpiece. These people had no idea the guy walking me through the home was the builder. But I knew. They were oohing and aahing at the design, materials, layout. But I was riveted by the man behind it all. I wanted to learn more about his brilliance, to figure out what makes him think and work the way he does.

I want to approach Jesus the same way. He is the master builder of our lives. But we aren't merely inanimate objects—planks of wood awaiting their use. No, we participate in our making (or unmaking, if you prefer).

> In a great house there are not only vessels of gold and silver but also of wood and clay, some for honorable use, some for dishonorable. Therefore, *if anyone cleanses [themselves]* from what is dishonorable, [they] will be a vessel for honorable use, set apart as holy, useful to the master of the house, ready for every good work. (2 Tim. 2:20–21, emphasis added)

Notice the opportunity to "cleanse" ourselves. What an amazing privilege. We're invited to join in the work of new creation. We don't have to be ignorant spectators, just passing through the home. We get to learn the ways of the builder and, by his Spirit, discover the beauty, significance, and glory of his work in and around us.

The One who "is the radiance of the glory of God and the exact imprint of his nature" (Heb. 1:3) is not ashamed to call us brothers and sisters. Is this simply because we now have his imputed righteousness (1 Cor. 5:21)? No! The truth is greater but not less than that. He is not ashamed to call us brothers and sisters because we now have his Spirit in us, positioning us to live like him and walk in the footsteps of true humanity. This is the otherness we're called to know. It's in his footsteps that we find the glory of being.

"Follow me," Jesus says.

## YOU, THE SAINT

I once spoke at a church in Texas for a friend of mine who is the executive pastor. Upon checking into the hotel, I found a note containing the following words:

> Your wisdom, humility, and courage challenge me to be a better son, husband, leader, and friend. You embody to me a Hebrews 11:38 man. The world is not worthy of men like you.

My first thought was, *Could I really belong to such a group?* I've always loved Hebrews 11. It's a list of men and women who disrupted our world by belonging to another. I forced my mind to do the humble thing and dismiss the pastor's kind words. I quickly reminded myself that I've never split the Red Sea or rescued a nation. But I could sense God was speaking to me through the note. There was something prophetic at work. God's Spirit was inviting me to be numbered among them.

Each of these greats—Moses, Enoch, Sarah, Daniel, and so on—chased the invisible. Their faith moved them beyond the limitations of their world, creating new playing fields for God to move in. They endured the struggle by seeing the One who is invisible. The world wasn't worthy of them, but they were exactly what this world needed. Their otherness was an impetus for change, glorious change. Their lives moved humanity toward the glory of the cross. And now because we are all found in Christ, you and I can join their number. We are invited to build for the kingdom (Heb. 11:39–12:2). We can become Hebrews 11 men and women!

Sadly, it's easier to fight our peculiarity than to build for the kingdom. This seems to be the tragic modus operandi of the people of God. It's why Israel wanted a king—they wanted to be like the other nations. An invisible king wasn't enough, and it was strange dealing with the unseen. They desired a mediator, a good-looking man who could bridge the gap between them and their peculiar God. They wanted a man who looked and smelled like them. Besides, you can't manipulate the invisible, but flesh and blood can be broken, exploited, and replaced when convenient.

Our God has always offered symbols for our peculiarity: circumcision, the Torah, and the Beatitudes, to name a few. Every symbol strangely glorious. Each one inviting us beyond conventional limitations. These symbols and practices are, essentially, pathways into a new way of being. Some of these practices had their season and fulfillment. Others still animate our lives today. But all of them remind us that there is more than what we now know, feel, and do. They welcome us into the transcendent—a way of being that escapes time, location, and culture. A glorious life marked by the otherness of the invisible God—the God whose ways are higher than ours because they are *other* than ours.

"To this [God] called you through our gospel, so that you may obtain the *glory* of our Lord Jesus Christ" (2 Thess. 2:14, emphasis added). Did you catch that? Your calling is to obtain the glory of Christ. Yes, the glory of Christ. In fact, it is his glory that unifies and marks his beautifully diverse Saints (John 17).

—I—

Our lives can and must disrupt the ways of the world, unveiling a new way to be human. The real and final evolution, if you will. The humanity that requires iteration upon iteration of death and surrender. The humanity that's brimming over with a life that knows no end. The humanity that reaches backward and forward, touching every tribe, nation, and tongue. This is the life and fraternity we were made for. It is an eternal life pulsing with the divine DNA that is uniquely expressed through each facet of God's good creation. This is the good life.

But none of this can become personal until you believe you were created for glory. Yes, you. Faith in general does you no good. Faith must become personal and specific. God gave his Son for *you*. Whether you like it or not, you're part of the story. No matter how much you kick or scream or deny, the narrative doesn't change. The story of glory is not about another place or time, and it's certainly not just about someone else. It's about your heart, your life, your people. Wherever you find yourself today, you are marked for glory.

"Throughout the coming ages, we will be the visible display of the infinite, limitless riches of his grace and kindness, which was showered upon us in Christ Jesus" (Eph. 2:7 TPT). The question is, Will you receive the fullness of grace, the fullness of Christ? Will you let go of the Old Self and be surprised by the New? My friend, there is nothing truly wonderful outside this path. You could call this the narrow road, the way to life. In this place of surrender, the Spirit of Christ works in you.

If you feel lost or disoriented, that's okay. All of us are traveling into something *other* than where we have been.

Ask for eyes to see. Ask for the Helper to guide you. Ask for the capacity to know. In your humility, you'll find strength—a strength to dive into fear, a strength to believe for something more, a strength to open yourself to the mystery of life.

In humble confidence, you will find the strength to participate in the beauty and wonder of the final day.

If you've made it this far, you can no longer deny who you are. After all, too whom much is given, much is required.

You are a Saint. Now become one.

> All your saints shall bless you!
> They shall speak of the glory of your kingdom
>     and tell of your power,
> to make known to the children of man your
>         mighty deeds,
>     and the glorious splendor of your kingdom.
> Your kingdom is an everlasting kingdom,
>     and your dominion endures throughout all
>         generations.
>
> Psalm 145:10–13

# ACKNOWLEDGMENTS

To the love of my life, Julianna, I wouldn't have been able to write this message without your faith, hope, and love. Everything that I am is yours.

To my children, Asher, Sophia, Elizabeth, and Augustus, thank you for opening my eyes to the Father's love. May each of you see up close what I have only seen in the distance.

To my parents, John and Lisa, your integrity, faithfulness, and love created a safe space for me to fail and grow. May my life always honor your legacy and passion.

To my brothers, Austin, J. Alexander, and Arden, you have loved and fought for me through the highs and lows. The way you honor me inspires me to be the older brother you deserve.

To my comrades at Messenger International, it's been one of the great joys of my life to labor with you over the years. Thank you for pushing me forward and making this message your own.

To Andrea, thank you for lending your experience, encouragement, and sharp eyes to this project. Your tender strength made what I thought would be an intimidating editing process rather enjoyable.

To Jen, Patti, Mark, Abby, Anna, Jane, and Gisèle, thank you for working tirelessly on these words and perfecting the aesthetic. I've loved every minute of our collaboration.

To Esther, Jill, Whitney, and the team at The FEDD Agency, your excitement and commitment throughout the whole creation process blew me away. Thank you for everything you've done for this message.

To my dear friends, extended family, and mentors, space doesn't allow me to mention you all by name, but you know who you are. Thank you for being my people. Your candor, support, and love make all the difference.

# APPENDIX

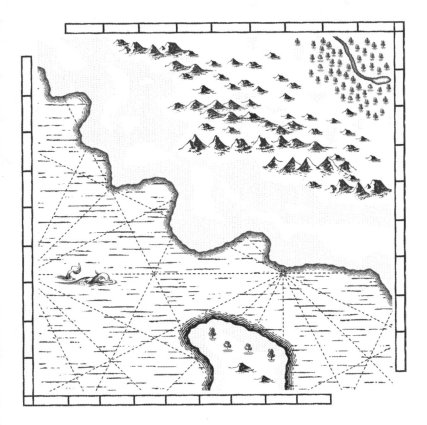

# NOTES

## Chapter 1  The Good Life

1. Eugene Peterson, *Run with the Horses: The Quest for Life at Its Best* (Downers Grove, IL: InterVarsity, 1983), 49.

2. E. F. Schumacher, *A Guide for the Perplexed* (New York: Perennial Library, 1977), 38.

3. N. T. Wright, *The Kingdom New Testament: A Contemporary Translation* (New York: HarperCollins, 2011), 19.

4. "She will bear a Son, and you shall call His name Jesus [the Greek form of the Hebrew Joshua, which means Savior], for He will save His people from their sins [that is, prevent them from failing and missing the true end and scope of life, which is God]" (Matt. 1:21 AMPC).

5. Heb. 2:5–18 and John 1:1–14.

6. This is a combination of Mark 10:17 and Matt. 19:16.

7. This is a combination of Mark 10:18 and Matt. 19:17.

8. This is a combination of Mark 10:19 and Matt. 19:19.

9. This is a combination of Mark 10:20 and Matt. 19:20.

10. Matt. 19:21.

11. Matt. 19:22.

12. Both Matt. 27 and Mark 15 explicitly state that both of the men crucified with Jesus hurled insults at him.

## Chapter 2  Saints

1. V. P. Furnish, "saints," in *HarperCollins Bible Dictionary*, ed. M. A. Powell, rev. and updated ed. (New York: HarperCollins, 2011), 906.

2. Walter A. Elwell and Philip W. Comfort, eds., *Tyndale Bible Dictionary*, Tyndale Reference Library (Wheaton: Tyndale, 2001), 1151.

3. Paraphrase of C. S. Lewis, *Mere Christianity* in *The Complete C. S. Lewis Signature Classics* (New York: HarperCollins, 2002), 170.

4. Lewis, *Mere Christianity*, 175–76.

5. Cathy Lynn Grossman, "Young Adults Aren't Sticking with Church," *USA Today*, August 8, 2007, https://usatoday30.usatoday.com/printedition/life/20070807/d_churchdropout07.art.htm.

## Chapter 3  Mirror, Mirror

1. John 1:1, note b, *The Passion Translation* (Savage, MN: Broadstreet Publishing, 2017), 579.

2. Dougan Clark, *The Theology of Holiness* (Gloucester, UK: Dodo Press, n.d.), 93.

3. Douglas J. Moo, *The Letter of James*, The Pillar New Testament Commentary (Grand Rapids: Eerdmans; Leicester, UK: Apollos, 2000), 90.

4. "Hubble's Mirror Flaw," NASA, last updated August 3, 2017, https://www.nasa.gov/content/hubbles-mirror-flaw.

## Chapter 4  To Fear or Not to Fear?

1. Isa. 11:2–3.

2. "Snakes Kill More Than 90,000 around the World," *Telegraph*, November 3, 2008, https://www.telegraph.co.uk/news/health/3372712/Snakes-kill-more-than-90000-around-the-world.html.

3. Exod. 19.

4. Adapted from J. I. Packer, *Knowing God*, 2nd ed. (London: Hodder and Stoughton, 1993), 138.

5. Adam Chandler, "Why Americans Lead the Way in Food Waste," *Atlantic*, July 15, 2016, https://www.theatlantic.com/business/archive/2016/07/american-food-waste/491513/.

6. William Barrett, *The Illusion of Technique* (Garden City, NY: Anchor Press/Doubleday, 1978), 219.

7. T. S. Eliot, "Choruses from the Rock," in *Collected Poems, 1909–1962* (Orlando, FL: Harcourt Brace, 1991), 147.

8. Adapted from George MacDonald, "Life," in *Unspoken Sermons*, Series 2, Classics Reprint Series (CreateSpace Independent Publishing, 2016).

9. N. T. Wright, *Simply Christian: Why Christianity Makes Sense* (New York: HarperCollins, 2006), 67.

10. Gary V. Smith, *Isaiah 1–39*, The New American Commentary, vol. 15A (Nashville: B&H, 2007), 190.

11. Rabbi Brian Bileci, a good friend of mine, shared this concept with me.

12. I was first introduced to this revelation in Rudolf Otto's book *The Idea of the Holy* (London: Oxford University Press, 1950), 26.

13. Elwell and Comfort, eds., *Tyndale Bible Dictionary*, 1150.

14. Smith, *Isaiah 1–39*, 191.

15. Otto, *Idea of the Holy*, 28.

16. "H. A. Williams," in *The God I Want*, ed. James Mitchell (London: Constable & Co, 1967), 180.

17. *Ein begriffener Gott ist kein Gott*, Gerhard Tersteegen (1697–1769), https://www.azquotes.com/quote/1132440.

### Chapter 5 Into Fear

1. *Merriam-Webster*, s.v. "intimate," accessed October 30, 2018, https://www.merriam-webster.com/dictionary/intimate.

2. 1 Cor. 13:1, note e, *The Passion Translation*, 833.

3. Lewis, *Mere Christianity*, 143.

4. Eugene Peterson, *Christ Plays in Ten Thousand Places: A Conversation in Spiritual Theology* (Grand Rapids: Eerdmans, 2008), 122.

### Chapter 6 The S★★ Word

1. W. Arndt, F. W. Danker, W. Bauer, and F. W. Gingrich, *A Greek-English Lexicon of the New Testament and Other Early Christian Literature*, 3rd ed. (Chicago: University of Chicago Press, 2000), 50.

2. AZ Quotes, accessed October 30, 2018, https://www.azquotes.com/quote/571986.

### Chapter 7 Worship

1. "A. Stephan Hopkinson," in *The God I Want*, 119.

2. Paraphrase of Lewis, *Mere Christianity*, 168.

3. Wright, *Simply Christian*, 236–37.

### Chapter 8 God's Love Language

1. Gary D. Chapman, *The 5 Love Languages: The Secret to Love That Lasts* (Chicago: Northfield Publishing, 1992).

2. My mom, the extraordinary Lisa Bevere, unpacks this revelation in her book *Girls with Swords: How to Carry Your Cross Like a Hero* (Colorado Springs: WaterBrook, 2013).

3. "Open yourself to my love" is my paraphrase of many of the verses found in the Psalms, the Prophets, and the Gospels. "My grace is sufficient for you" is from 2 Cor. 12:9.

4. G. Kittel, G. W. Bromiley, and G. Friedrich, eds., *Theological Dictionary of the New Testament*, vol. 3 (Grand Rapids: Eerdmans, 1964), 922.

5. Jean Vanier, *Becoming Human* (Mahwah, NJ: Paulist Press, 1998), 22.

6. N. T. Wright, "People of Hope: John 20:19–End," a sermon for the ecumenical service, October 20, 2011, https://www.irishchurches.org/cmsfiles/resources/Reports/IICM11_NT_Wright__Sermon_People_of_hope__20_october_2011.pdf.

7. MacDonald, "The Displeasure of Jesus," in *Unspoken Sermons*, Series 3.

8. N. T. Wright, *Hebrews for Everyone* (London: Society for Promoting Christian Knowledge, 2004), 48–49.

9. 1 Cor. 13:1, note e, *The Passion Translation*, 833, emphasis added.

## Chapter 9  Back to Life

1. Anthony de Mello, *The Song of the Bird* (New York: Doubleday, 1982), 96.

2. Nadia Kounang, "What Is the Science behind Fear?," CNN, October 29, 2015, https://www.cnn.com/2015/10/29/health/science-of-fear/index.html.

3. 1 Cor. 1:3, note c, *The Passion Translation*, 801.

4. Dietrich Bonhoeffer, *The Wisdom and Witness of Dietrich Bonhoeffer* (Minneapolis: Augsburg Fortress, 2000), 44.

5. A. W. Tozer, *Jesus: The Life and Ministry of God the Son—Collected Insights from A. W. Tozer* (Chicago: Moody, 2017), 27.

6. Thomas Keating, *Intimacy with God: An Introduction to Centering Prayer* (New York: Crossroad, 2009), 54–55.

## Chapter 10  Glory

1. N. T. Wright, *How God Became King: The Forgotten Story of the Gospels* (New York: HarperCollins, 2012), 227.

2. Paraphrased from Gary V. Smith, *Isaiah 40–66,* The New American Commentary, vol. 15B (Nashville: B&H, 2009), 613.

3. Charles Haddon Spurgeon, *Gleanings Among the Sheaves* (1869), 57, https://www.azquotes.com/quote/703877.

4. Francis Frangipane, *Holiness, Truth, and the Presence of God* (Lake Mary, FL: Charisma House, 2011), 21.

5. Thomas Aquinas, *Summa Theologica*, II-II, q. 24, a. 3, ad. 2.

**Addison D. Bevere** is a man who appreciates the simple things in life—time spent playing with his four kids, late-night conversations with his wife, interesting words that no one uses, a meaningful day of work, and, of course, a good book. Addison is also the COO of Messenger International, an organization that impacts millions of people in over 150 countries through its various initiatives, and the cofounder of SonsAndDaughters.tv. To learn more about him, visit AddisonBevere.com.

## STAY ENGAGED WITH *SAINTS* AND ADDISON BEVERE

ADDISONBEVERE.COM

#SAINTSBOOK

## LET'S TALK ABOUT BOOKS

- Share or mention the book on your social media platforms. Use the hashtag **#SAINTSbook**.

- Write a book review on your blog or on a retailer site.

- Pick up a copy for friends, family, or anyone who you think would enjoy and be challenged by its message!

- Share this message on Twitter or Instagram:
  **I loved #SAINTSbook by @addisonbevere // @RevellBooks**

- Share this message on Facebook:
  **I loved #SAINTSbook by @addisondbevere // @RevellBooks**

- Recommend this book for your church, workplace, book club, or small group.

- Follow Revell on social media and tell us what you like.

 RevellBooks

 RevellBooks

 RevellBooks